International Economic Consequences of High-Priced Energy

A Statement on National Policy
by the Research and Policy Committee
of the Committee for Economic Development

September 1975

Prepared in association with
CEDA Committee for Economic Development of Australia
CEPES European Committee for Economic and Social Progress
(West Germany)
IDEP Institut de l'Entreprise (France)
KEIZAI DOYUKAI Japan Committee for Economic Development
PEP Political and Economic Planning (Britain)
SNS Industrial Council for Social and Economic Studies
(Sweden)

Library of Congress Cataloging in Publication Data

Committee for Economic Development.
   International economic consequences of high-
priced energy.

   1. Energy policy.   2. International economic
relations.   3. Balance of payments.   I. Title.
HD9502.A2C64   1975   333.7   75-22468
ISBN 0-87186-759-1   lib. bdg.
ISBN 0-87186-059-7   pbk.

First printing: September 1975
Paperbound: $2.50
Library binding: $4.00
Printed in the United States of America by Georgian Press, Inc.
Design: Harry Carter

COMMITTEE FOR ECONOMIC DEVELOPMENT
477 Madison Avenue, New York, N.Y. 10022

Contents

Responsibility for CED Statements on National Policy

The Committee for Economic Development is an independent research and educational organization of two hundred business executives and educators. CED is nonprofit, nonpartisan, and nonpolitical. Its purpose is to propose policies that will help to bring about steady economic growth at high employment and reasonably stable prices, increase productivity and living standards, provide greater and more equal opportunity for every citizen, and improve the quality of life for all. A more complete description of the objectives and organization of CED is to be found in the section beginning on page 104.

All CED policy recommendations must have the approval of the Research and Policy Committee, a group of sixty trustees whose names are listed on these pages. This Committee is directed under the bylaws to "initiate studies into the principles of business policy and of public policy which will foster the full contribution by industry and commerce to the attainment and maintenance" of the objectives stated above. The bylaws emphasize that "all research is to be thoroughly objective in character, and the approach in each instance is to be from the standpoint of the general welfare and not from that of any special political or economic group." The Committee is aided by a Research Advisory Board of leading social scientists and by a small permanent professional staff.

The Research and Policy Committee offers this statement as an aid in bringing about greater understanding of the origins and impact of the

4

international energy crisis, its domestic implications, and its effect on international finance and trade policy and on the economies of the developing nations. The Committee is not attempting to pass judgment on any pending specific legislative proposals; its purpose is to urge careful consideration of the objectives set forth in the statement and of the best means of accomplishing those objectives.

Each statement on national policy is preceded by discussions, meetings, and exchanges of memoranda, often stretching over many months. The research is undertaken by a subcommittee, assisted by advisors chosen for their competence in the field under study. The members and advisors of the International Energy Project Subcommittee, which prepared this statement, are listed on page 6.

The full Research and Policy Committee participates in the drafting of findings and recommendations. Likewise, the trustees on the drafting subcommittee vote to approve or disapprove a policy statement, and they share with the Research and Policy Committee the privilege of submitting individual comments for publication, as noted on this and the following page and on the appropriate page of the text of the statement.

Except for the members of the Research and Policy Committee and the responsible subcommittee, the recommendations presented herein are not necessarily endorsed by other trustees or by the advisors, contributors, staff members, or others associated with CED.

6

Purpose of This Statement

THE SHOCKS AND REPERCUSSIONS produced by sharply rising international energy costs have placed great strains on the world's market economies. As recent events have demonstrated, nations whose industrial economic activities are closely linked to a reliable supply of imported petroleum at reasonable prices are hard hit by inflation when supplies become uncertain and prices are abruptly increased. Higher oil prices breed higher prices for goods and services that depend on oil and rising demands from workers for higher wages to pay for those goods and services. Through this process, inflation moves ever higher, threatening the growth of production and employment.

The CED Research and Policy Committee has long been concerned about the economic implications of energy and raw materials supplies. Recognizing the increasing reliance of the United States on imported oil as a source of energy, the Committee authorized a project in the spring of 1973 that led to publication last year of the statement *Achieving Energy Independence*. That statement recommended a national energy policy for the United States that would, through conservation, substitution, and domestic production, substantially reduce the country's dependence on imported fuel.

Global Setting. But national energy policies must be formulated in a global setting. With this in mind, the Committee joined with six foreign counterparts in sponsoring the First World Symposium on Energy and Raw Materials in Paris in June 1974. The symposium, which brought together more than a thousand participants from both producing and consuming countries, assessed the impact of declining fuel and raw material resources and rising prices on consumption, living standards, global political relationships, and international trade and finance. The success

7

of this effort encouraged the sponsoring groups to continue to examine together some of the critical issues raised at the Paris meeting. Thus, they immediately embarked on a joint project that led to the present statement.

International Economic Consequences of High-Priced Energy is the result of a year of joint study and discussion by the Committee and similar private-sector organizations in France, Germany, the United Kingdom, Sweden, Australia, and Japan. Through this cooperation, participants from the seven organizations agreed on the positions presented in the statement, subject to the exceptions indicated in the footnotes. A listing of the international committees that cooperated in the study appears on pages 111 to 113.

The statement is a blueprint for cooperative action to deal with the international economic consequences of a quadrupling of oil prices by the Organization of Petroleum Exporting Countries (OPEC) in late 1973 and other forces that precipitated a global energy crisis. Recent warnings from OPEC of yet another round of oil-price increases underscores the urgency for oil-consuming countries to develop policies that will reduce their vulnerability to such threats.

The statement does not attempt to enumerate the various domestic policies needed to withstand the effects of supply cutbacks or price increases in individual countries. For the United States, such policies were recommended in *Achieving Energy Independence*, but most of the government actions required to launch a comprehensive U.S. energy program have yet to be taken. Further delay will make it more difficult for the United States to meet its own long-term energy requirements and to make an effective contribution to international solutions.

Cooperation among Industrial Countries. The present statement addresses the origins and impact of the international energy crisis, its domestic economic implications, and its effects on international finance and trade policy and on the economies of the developing nations. It calls for cooperation among the industrial countries in planning for emergency conservation and fuel allocation, in developing new sources of supply, and in mitigating economic damage to the countries most affected by high oil prices.

The statement emphasizes the importance of the health and vitality of the economies of oil-importing countries as a determining factor in their ability to withstand the pressure of higher oil prices. It urges the member countries of the Organization for Economic Cooperation and

Development (OECD) to place primary emphasis on long-term policies for stimulating investment as a means of financing the burden of higher energy costs.

In the area of international finance, the statement endorses measures to deal with difficulties arising from the huge flows of surplus earnings of some OPEC countries into world financial centers. As a last resort in financing deficits of industrial nations, it supports the concept of a mutual aid fund, or "safety net," for OECD countries, through which financially stronger countries would provide credit or credit guarantees to financially weaker ones. As for the developing countries, the statement urges action both by the World Bank and the International Monetary Fund and by OPEC and OECD in offering the poorest nations assistance (through interest subsidies and other arrangements) in meeting their foreign exchange requirements.

Recognizing that politically motivated export restrictions, such as the 1973 oil embargo, are not covered by present rules governing international trade policy, the statement calls for new international rules that would clearly define and circumscribe export controls at least in situations of short supply. It suggests exploration of multilateral arrangements on certain internationally traded commodities for moderating sharp fluctuations in prices of primary products and in preventing arbitrary interruptions of supply, and it views with cautious optimism the eventual possibility of an international commodity agreement involving the principal exporters and importers of petroleum.

Acknowledgments. On behalf of the Research and Policy Committee, I express deep appreciation to the participants from the following counterpart groups who worked tirelessly with CED in the spirit of friendship, cooperation, and mutual understanding that has characterized our joint efforts over many years: the French Institut de l'Entreprise (IDEP), the German CEPES (European Committee for Economic and Social Progress), the British PEP (Political and Economic Planning), the Swedish SNS (Industrial Council for Social and Economic Studies), the Committee for Economic Development of Australia (CEDA), and Keizai Doyukai (Japan Committee for Economic Development). Such cooperation between CED and organizations with similar objectives has been instrumental in enabling the private sector in the United States and other industrial nations to formulate common policies on a wide range of international economic issues. The Committee is especially indebted to William H. Franklin, retired board chairman of Caterpillar Tractor Company and chairman of CED, who provided leadership as chairman of the CED Subcommittee on the International Energy Project, and to the skilled and experienced members of his subcommittee, whose names appear on page 6. Isaiah Frank, William L. Clayton Professor of International Economics at the Johns Hopkins University School of Advanced International Studies and director of international economic studies for CED, deserves special recognition as project director for the successful completion of this policy statement in so brief a time. This study was supported by a grant from the Richard King Mellon Foundation, whose assistance in funding this and CED's earlier energy study is greatly appreciated.

Philip M. Klutznick, *Chairman*
Research and Policy Committee

Chapter 1

Introduction and Summary
of Recommendations

INCREASES IN INTERNATIONAL OIL PRICES and the manipulation of supplies have caused an unprecedented upheaval in the world economy. It is our hope that world oil prices can be reduced. But present price levels have created new and massive economic problems,* and these can be manageable only if our governments develop a wide array of measures to deal with the situation and mobilize the public support needed to translate those measures into action. This will require vigorous government leadership in finding solutions through both domestic programs and international cooperation.*

 THE CED RESEARCH AND POLICY COMMITTEE notes that this policy statement is a joint effort on the part of the Committee and its foreign counterpart organizations to reach a common assessment of the economic consequences of high energy prices and an agreed program of *international cooperative action* to deal with those consequences. The statement does not attempt to address the many issues involved in designing a *national* energy policy for the United States, including domestic measures to encourage conservation, storage, and the development of new sources of supply. CED has dealt with these matters in a separate policy statement, *Achieving Energy Independence,* published in December 1974. That statement examined the factors, including counterproductive public policies, that led to the energy problem; it recommended measures that could bring domestic energy production and consumption into better balance. The desired result of these policies should be an oil-import level of no more than 10 percent of total energy consumption by 1985 and the ability to withstand any embargo that might occur before then.

See memorandum by *THEODORE O. YNTEMA, page 90.

* **INSTITUT DE L'ENTREPRISE (IDEP,** France) wishes to pay tribute to the achievement of the participants in this project who drew up this statement dealing with a difficult subject on which the various national groups frequently held divergent views arising from the differing situations in which various countries find themselves as regards energy supplies. This is well illustrated by the statement *Achieving Energy Independence* referred to by CED and which corresponds to the particular situation of the United States. The French group placed particular emphasis in preliminary studies on three points:

First, given the complexity of the problem and the fact that it can evolve sharply, it would be difficult for any paper prepared several months prior to publication to reflect the precise views of its authors at the time of publication, since these are subject to modification because of unforeseen circumstances. This comment is, however, to be taken in its general sense, and the whole statement had the agreement in principle of IDEP at the end of June 1975, when the statement was drafted in its final form, with the very few exceptions indicated by footnotes.

Second, the idea of the study was decided upon jointly at the completion of a symposium on energy and raw materials held in Paris in June 1974. It was clear that work would concentrate only on effects of increased prices of energy products, and this is in fact the question dealt with by the jointly agreed text. Needless to say, therefore, anything relating to other raw materials and more generally to the inflationary climate in which we have to exist was excluded from the study to be found here. Again, however, neither of these two factors has been overlooked in the background discussions of the work carried out, even if they are not referred to systematically, and this is something the critical reader should bear in mind.

Third, French national policy is comparatively dissimilar to that of the other OECD countries, if not in terms of basic principles and objectives, then in terms of the particulars of the procedure advocated for implementing international cooperation. It has not always been easy in a paper with a sharply defined objective (as indicated above) either to allow for such differences or to clarify or explain them. IDEP, however, declares itself content with the manner in which its observations have been accepted and the comprehension manifested by other delegations. This is readily gathered from a perusal of the various preliminary drafts.

✳ CEDA (Australia) agrees with the policy statement except for the question of financial institutions, as stated in our footnote on pages 25 and 53.

Substantial international responses have already occurred among the oil-importing countries, and there is broad scope for constructive cooperation between oil-exporting and oil-importing countries. The importing countries require stable oil supplies at reasonable prices; the exporting countries aspire to economic development, a goal that can only be realized with the technical help of the industrial countries. Both the oil-exporting countries and the industrial countries need a healthy, growing world economy, which in turn requires their assistance to the developing countries that are not oil producers. Even under the most optimistic circumstances, however, there will continue to be severe strains on the world economy. These strains will be felt with special force in the developing countries.

The immediate necessity is to restore domestic economic growth and to adjust the international economy to the new situation, particularly to the consequences of the explosive rise in the price of oil charged by members of the Organization of Petroleum Exporting Countries (OPEC). In the medium and longer term, it is in the interests of oil-importing countries to attempt to lower the world price of oil* through conservation and the development of alternative supplies and to endeavor to ensure that their economies are never again so vulnerable to the export policies of a small group of countries. This policy statement concentrates on international cooperative action to deal with the immediate objectives but also considers the medium- and longer-term goals.**

ORIGINS AND IMPACT
OF THE INTERNATIONAL ENERGY CRISIS

Although the crisis of late 1973 can be traced directly to actions taken by the oil-exporting countries, many forces lie behind the changes that have occurred. Even before the shock of politically motivated supply

See memorandum by *R. HEATH LARRY, page 90.
See memoranda by **R. HEATH LARRY, page 91, by G. BARRON MALLORY, page 92, and by JAMES Q. RIORDAN, page 93.

cutbacks and embargoes, it had become increasingly clear that an energy crisis lay ahead unless appropriate actions to avert it were initiated. The problem arose basically from the rapid growth of world energy consumption, the shift from coal to petroleum, and the growing dependence of industrial countries on imported energy, which increasingly meant Middle East petroleum.

Shift in Power. As a result of these developments and the shift in market power that they brought about, decisions on the production, marketing, and pricing of oil have increasingly reflected the interests of the oil-exporting countries. This has necessarily affected the role of the international oil companies. The shift in power relationships has gathered momentum since 1970 and reached its climax in 1973 in the wake of the October War in the Middle East, when all pretense of negotiating with the oil companies was abandoned. Acting in concert under the aegis of OPEC, the producing countries quadrupled the price of oil in the last three months of 1973, an action that has had major repercussions on the world economic and financial system.

Some substantial increase in oil prices may well have been justified, and if that increase had been spread out over a period of years, it could have been smoothly accommodated by the rest of the world. However, the abruptness and the steepness of the increase (see Figure 1)* contributed to a major international economic crisis. For a number of months in 1973 and 1974, the oil crisis included two additional elements: politically motivated supply cutbacks so severe that markets were prevented from clearing even at the new prices and embargoes on the shipment of oil to particular consuming countries whose Middle East policies were considered hostile to the Arab cause.

The role of the international oil companies in the producing countries has been progressively reduced to that of buying crude oil and providing technical services. But the change in power relationships goes far beyond the reshaped role of the oil companies. The governments of the principal oil-producing countries now have the capacity to exert concerted market power and to use that power for political as well as economic purposes.

A number of oil-consuming countries are now threatened with economic stagnation and possibly severe disruption because of their inability to pay higher oil-import bills. At the same time, a number of OPEC members are earning sums vastly in excess of their ability to spend or invest at home. This poses the complex economic and political problems

See memorandum by *R. HEATH LARRY, page 93.

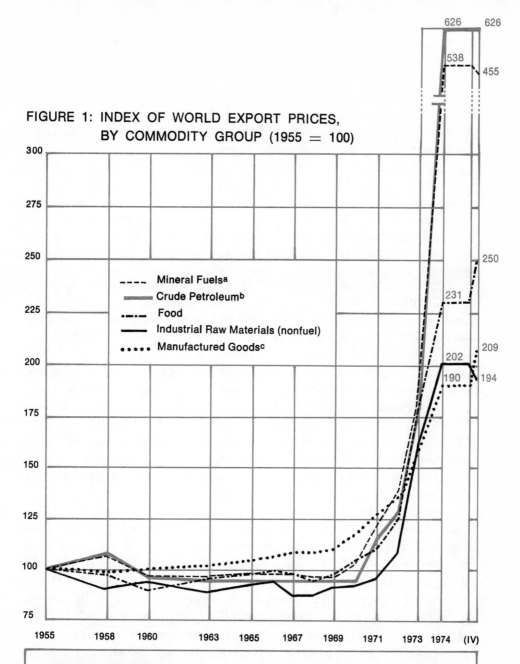

FIGURE 1: INDEX OF WORLD EXPORT PRICES,
BY COMMODITY GROUP (1955 = 100)

Legend:
- - - - Mineral Fuels[a]
▬▬▬ Crude Petroleum[b]
-·-·- Food
──── Industrial Raw Materials (nonfuel)
•••• Manufactured Goods[c]

a Includes crude petroleum.
b Data are for Middle East Gulf light and are based on posted prices. The posted price is a reference price used as a basis for calculating the government's take (royalty and tax payments) in oil-producing countries. During the late 1950s and 1960s, government take as a percentage of posted price rose slightly, averaging about 50 percent over the period. Then, beginning in 1971, as a result of participation and increases in royalty and tax rates, the percentage of government take rose sharply, reaching a level of about 90 percent in the fourth quarter of 1974.
c Based on unit value indexes.
SOURCES: UN, *Monthly Bulletin of Statistics;* and UN, *Price Movements of Basic Commodities in International Trade, 1950–1970* (1972).

15

of dealing with the resulting world imbalance in current payments and of managing an accumulation of OPEC claims on the rest of the world on a scale unprecedented in recent history.

Steps must be taken immediately to develop alternative sources of supplies, but the effect of these measures will not be generally felt for some time. Thus, in the short run, conservation is the main measure that oil-importing countries can employ to apply downward pressure on the price of imported oil. But for the next several years, the price of oil may well stay high, and this must be taken into account in national and international policy making.

Changes in World Payments. Higher oil prices have produced a dramatic change in the pattern of world payments. Prior to the price increases of late 1973, the industrial countries as a group typically earned a balance-of-payments surplus on current account of about $12 billion. The developing countries experienced a deficit of comparable magnitude, and this was accommodated by the flow of aid and capital to them.

That situation has changed drastically. In 1974, the developed countries as a group shifted to a current account deficit of almost $34 billion; the deficit of those developing countries that are not oil producers amounted to some $22 billion. At the same time, the oil-exporting countries have had a tenfold increase in their current account surplus, from $6 billion in 1973 to more than $60 billion in 1974.

Undoubtedly, the oil exporters as a group will continue to accumulate substantial current account surpluses at least through 1980, and these surpluses will inevitably result in corresponding current account deficits in many of the industrial and developing countries. Opinions differ on the scale and trend of these surpluses and deficits because many factors are involved, including the future course of petroleum prices, the volume of OPEC oil exports, the trend in OPEC exports other than oil, the rate at which the OPEC countries can step up their capacity to absorb imports, the trend in the prices of OPEC imports, and the rate of return on OPEC foreign investments.

The Organization for Economic Cooperation and Development (OECD) and the World Bank have been among the principal international organizations involved in estimating the OPEC surpluses. Both have projected diminishing annual surpluses between 1974 and 1980 in constant dollars. In making its projection, OECD has taken the differing import capacities of OPEC countries into account; it has assumed that the real price of imported crude oil will remain at the level reached at the end of 1974 and that the volume of OECD oil imports in 1980 will be approximately the same as the 1974 level as a consequence of reduced growth in energy consumption and higher domestic production. Thus, OECD has estimated that the cumulative OPEC surplus in 1980 will be between $200 and $250 billion in constant 1974 dollars. A revised World Bank projection falls somewhat below the middle of that range. If the bank's price forecasts are used to adjust for inflation,[1] the OECD estimate of the cumulative 1980 OPEC surplus in current dollars amounts to between $330 and $413 billion.[2] However, the increase in imports by OPEC countries has been more rapid than was originally foreseen, and most recent estimates of future OPEC surpluses represent substantial downward revisions of those made in mid-1974. Furthermore, it should be remembered that all such estimates are subject to a wide margin of error because of the uncertainties surrounding the principal variables involved.

DOMESTIC ECONOMIC IMPLICATIONS

The capacity of importing countries to absorb the burden of higher oil prices depends, first of all, on the health and vitality of their own economies. When the huge oil-price increases occurred, many OECD countries were already plagued by the twin economic problems of high inflation and weakness in production. The increases have exacerbated both problems and have greatly complicated the task of domestic economic management.

Inflation. The OPEC action has given increased impetus to inflation in two ways: first, by directly increasing the price of a product as basic as petroleum and indirectly increasing prices for all other forms of energy and, second, by stimulating higher wage demands from workers seeking to protect their incomes from erosion by rising prices. The increased oil

---

[1] The average inflation rate for the period from 1974 to 1980 is projected at 8.8 percent, but it is based on a pattern of annual rates that decline over the period to 7.0 percent in 1980.

[2] Scenarios resulting in substantially lower estimates have been published by others, including the Morgan Guaranty Trust Company of New York and First National City Bank.

prices imply a deterioration in the terms of trade and a consequent overall loss of real income for each importing country. To the extent that particular groups within an importing country seek to avoid sharing in this loss, the burden is passed on to other groups, who may in turn react in ways that prolong the inflationary spiral. The tendency to resist such sharing has been accentuated by the income shifts associated with earlier and continuing inflation, and the dangers are consequently greater. *Among the urgent tasks facing the governments of importing countries is that of educating their people about the true dimensions and implications of the energy problem and the consequent need for restraint in demands for income adjustments.*

Output and Employment. Paradoxically, while high oil prices gave a new boost to worldwide inflationary pressures, they also dealt a severely depressing blow to world output and employment, which were already weakened. In the OECD countries, real GNP increased by 6.3 percent in 1973 but declined by 0.1 percent in 1974; little improvement is expected in 1975. The steep decline in the growth rate in 1974 was partly a consequence of the higher oil prices that absorbed purchasing power and thus reduced real aggregate demand for other goods and services. Some of this diverted purchasing power is being used by OPEC for increased imports of goods and services from the rest of the world. But approximately $60 billion was surplus to OPEC's needs in 1974, a figure generally indicative of the initial depressing effect on world output and employment.

Clearly, one of the first tasks of the governments of the OECD countries is to counter domestic economic stagnation, which has been exacerbated by oil-price increases and which has resulted in tremendous human suffering and waste of resources. The extent of this problem varies widely among OECD countries, and the precise mix of policies for stimulating the domestic economy while combating inflation must necessarily be adapted to the particular circumstances of each country. However, the closest consultation among the industrialized countries is desirable because expansionary policies stimulate an increase in imports and, if pursued in isolation, can lead to a prompt deterioration of any one country's balance-of-payments position.

In designing expansionary fiscal and monetary policies to offset the depressing impact of oil-price increases, countries have a choice of stimulating either consumption or investment or both. During the present recession, a substantial stimulus to both is clearly required. Ultimately, however, primary emphasis on encouraging consumption would contribute little to the long-term ability of oil-importing countries to finance the real burden of higher energy costs. **As OECD countries move closer to full employment, therefore, we recommend that government policies lean toward greater stimulus to investment (e.g., through more liberal depreciation allowances and investment credits).** In the last analysis, increased output resulting from new productive capacity will help the OECD countries to pay off their growing debt to the members of OPEC. Alternatively, the OECD countries will be able to reduce the growth of that debt by investing in other sources of energy, thereby achieving greater independence from OPEC supplies.

INTERNATIONAL FINANCIAL ISSUES*

Now that the supply cutbacks and destination embargoes have been relaxed, the major consequences of the OPEC countries' growth in power result from the increases in the price of oil. The revenues received by producer governments per barrel of oil at the end of 1974 amounted to about $10.00 for the Persian Gulf states,[3] which produce about two-thirds of the OPEC total, and more for most other producers. On this basis, the oil-export revenues of OPEC governments have escalated from less than $30 billion in 1973 to about $110 billion in 1974. When expenditures for imports of current goods and services were deducted from these increased revenues, the producing countries had a surplus of about $60 billion in 1974.

OPEC countries have two basic options for using their vastly increased oil revenues. They can import additional goods and services, or they can acquire assets in the rest of the world. To the extent that they increase their imports, the rest of the world will have a somewhat lower

---

[3] On equity oil (i.e., company-owned oil), taxes and royalties per barrel rose from about $.90 in 1970 to some $3.00 in October 1973 and then to $7.00 by January 1974 for light Arabian "marker crude" f.o.b. Ras Tanura. This was followed by further increases in tax and royalty rates that brought government revenues to about $9.80 per barrel of equity oil by December 1974. In addition, the governments earn a larger revenue per barrel on the portion of the oil that represents their share of ownership in the oil companies' producing operations. Most of the producing countries have the equivalent of at least 60 percent participation and a sale price for this oil equal to about 93 percent of the posted price (i.e., tax-reference price), for a realization of about $10.50. Thus, for the total operation, the average government income for the Persian Gulf states was about $10.00 per barrel.

See memorandum by *R. HEATH LARRY, page 93.

standard of living than it would otherwise have had because it will have to give up more real resources to pay for the same amount of oil or less. (If the entire increase in the proceeds of OPEC oil were spent annually on current imports, the transfer would amount to about 2 percent of the annual GNP of the OECD countries.) But, by the same token, the current payments problem of the rest of the world is relieved as exports to OPEC countries grow. However, the oil exporters as a group cannot presently absorb all the goods and services that their extra revenues can buy; therefore, they must acquire assets in the rest of the world. Although the sacrifice of real income in the oil-importing countries will thereby be currently reduced, the deficits in their balance of payments on current account will be increased, and more of their assets will be owned by OPEC nations.

In considering the prospects for OPEC absorption of additional imports, it is useful to divide the member countries into two groups. The first group (Saudi Arabia, Kuwait, the United Arab Emirates, Libya, and Qatar) is made up of countries that have small populations, large oil reserves, and limited natural resources other than oil. These countries, which have a total population of around 12 million, experienced net outflows of capital even before the recent growth of oil revenues. Moreover, their official monetary reserves at the end of 1972 amounted to almost twice their imports in that year, suggesting the absence of compelling internal pressures for the prompt use of foreign exchange to acquire imports. The second group (Indonesia, Iran, Iraq, Nigeria, Algeria, Venezuela, and Ecuador) consists of countries that have relatively large populations, more diversified resources, and more articulated development programs. These countries, which have a total population of about 270 million, were all net recipients of external capital as recently as 1972 and had international reserve assets equal to only half a year's imports, indicating strong pressures to translate foreign exchange earnings into imports.

OPEC receipts from petroleum exports have been rather evenly divided between these two groups. However, the future disposition of foreign exchange receipts will differ sharply between them. For the first group, the low absorbers, the rate at which imports can be increased will lag far behind the rate at which oil earnings will accumulate. At least in the near future, therefore, these countries will have no alternative but to use their additional oil revenues to expand their roles as net exporters of capital, in the form of either reserve accumulations or other types of international investment. However, countries in the second group should be able to use substantial portions of their increased oil revenues to expand imports for both domestic investment and domestic consumption. They will probably also retire some of their external debt and build up their monetary reserves, although not as extensively as the first group. Because disbursements will lag behind the preparation of new development projects in the near term, substantial sums are also likely to be available from this group for investment abroad.

One way or another, the increased flow of payments to the oil exporters will equal the increased flow from them in payment for imports and foreign assets. Unfortunately, however, the automatic matching of payments and receipts for the oil importers as a group does not occur automatically for each of them individually at acceptable levels of economic activity. Assuring an individual country of the capacity to finance its oil-import needs is of crucial importance not only to the country concerned but also to the efficient functioning of the international economic system as a whole.

Balance-of-Payments Adjustment. In the short run, the OECD countries as a group have no option but to accept a substantial deterioration in their current account that has to be offset by increases in capital inflows. Individual countries, however, may attempt to minimize their deficits by means of domestic deflation, exchange rate depreciation, or trade measures designed to discourage imports or stimulate exports. Considering the constraints on the ability of oil exporters to increase their imports in the short run, the main result of such measures is to shift the payments problem from one importing country to another. Pursued unilaterally, such measures could lead to destructive and self-defeating trade rivalry and worldwide economic depression. This danger is particularly acute in the light of the massive current account deficits experienced by several OECD countries in 1974.

As a practical approach to the problem of balance-of-payments adjustment for the OECD countries, we recommend that each country accept its narrowly defined oil-induced current deficit in the short run (say, 1975 and 1976) and attempt to finance this deficit through private and official capital flows from abroad. Deficits not directly related to oil-price increases should, of course, be corrected promptly. After 1976, as the long-term investment of OPEC surpluses settles into more stable patterns, we would suggest a gradual shift to greater reliance on correction of the remaining deficits on current account plus long-term capital accounts through exchange rate adjustments.

However, there is great need for close and frequent consultation among the financial officials of the principal trading nations with a view to agreeing on consistent balance-of-payments objectives. Account needs to be taken in these consultations of differences in the internal economic conditions of individual countries, in the balance-of-payments impact of higher oil prices, and in the ability to attract foreign capital on market terms.

OECD and the International Monetary Fund (IMF) are the appropriate forums for the kind of consultation envisaged here because they have an established record of concern for the consistency of the balance-of-payments aims and policies of their member countries. We believe that the present strains on the international financial system make such co-operation more urgent than ever.

Recycling OPEC Financial Surpluses. Consultations of the kind we have described should contribute to a more acceptable international distribution of current account deficits among oil-consuming countries. The objective of recycling is to ensure a pattern of capital flows that matches this distribution. Insofar as OPEC countries lend to or directly invest in oil-importing countries in proportion to their current account deficits, the need to recycle is minimized. But to the extent that the initial flows of capital from the oil exporters go excessively to some countries and insufficiently to others, secondary flows of capital among oil-consuming countries are needed.

In 1974, most of the surplus oil revenues flowed into the Eurocurrency market and into the traditional national money markets, especially New York and London. Lesser amounts went to European countries other than the United Kingdom and to Japan in the form of direct loans to official and semiofficial agencies, were transferred to developing countries directly or through multilateral lending institutions, or were invested in the private sector in the form of equities or real estate.

Banks operating in the Eurocurrency market served as the main vehicles for recycling oil money to countries that needed it to cover their deficits. In 1974, this private intermediation system ran up against a number of severe restraints. Oil-exporting countries tend to deposit their funds at short term; whereas deficit countries need credit at medium or long term. When the sums involved are so large and the deposits are held by only a few foreign governments, the risks may become unacceptable. Declining capital ratios of banks and the possibility of abrupt switches among currencies have added to the concern about risk and exposure. In this situation, banks have attempted to achieve greater stability by reducing the interest paid on short-term deposits and increasing the rate charged on longer-term loans. Nevertheless, some banks, particularly in the Eurocurrency market, may find themselves in a liquidity squeeze. **We strongly endorse the joint policy announced by the monetary authorities of the principal industrial countries that "means are available ... and will be used if and when necessary" to help banks in the Eurocurrency system that get into trouble through a sudden shift of funds.**[4]

The most serious limitation of private intermediation is that banks receiving funds from OPEC countries are understandably reluctant to lend them to governments and private borrowers in countries (whether developed or less developed) that have weak economies, heavy debt burdens, and poor payments prospects. Inevitably, therefore, a considerable part of oil deficits will have to be financed through official channels.

In considering official financial mechanisms for assisting economically weak countries to pay their oil-import bills, several guidelines are applicable. First, insofar as OECD countries assume the ultimate credit risk for loans or guarantees to each other, these countries should be in a position to set their own terms and conditions for such assistance rather than be subject to conditions laid down in organizations with wider membership. Second, special finance on an adequate scale should be provided for the developing countries, especially those most severely affected, primarily through expanding the operations of existing multilateral institutions, especially IMF and the World Bank, in which they are full participants. Third, because both OPEC and OECD countries have an interest in a healthy world economy, they should equitably share the risk of lending to countries in weak financial positions.

In recent months, considerable progress has been achieved in putting these principles into practice. The IMF oil facility, a special fund established on a scale of about $4 billion for 1974, was renewed in 1975 for more than $6 billion. Its funds are borrowed mainly from the oil-exporting countries and loaned to importing countries, mostly in the less developed world, for an average term of five years and in amounts related to the increase in their oil-import bills. An important innovation in 1975 will

---

[4] Bank for International Settlements, press review (Basel: September 10, 1974).

be an interest subsidy on the $1.3 to $1.7 billion that IMF estimates the thirty or so poorest developing countries will receive from the facility. **We welcome the extension of the IMF oil facility, particularly the establishment of the interest-subsidy arrangement for the least creditworthy developing countries. We call upon our governments as well as those of the OPEC countries to provide promptly the modest sums required to enable the interest-subsidy arrangement to function at full scale. We also urge sympathetic consideration of the extension of the facility on a scale appropriate to needs as they arise.** If the interest-subsidy arrangement is continued beyond 1975, consideration should be given to financing part of it through the sale by IMF in the market of a minor portion of its gold holdings, which are valued officially at $6.5 billion but which have a current market value of $26 billion. To conform with the Articles of Agreement, the sale would technically have to take place through one of the fund's members.

For financing industrial countries' deficits on current account, agreement has been reached on a $25 billion mutual aid fund, or "safety net," to be set up within the OECD framework and to be used as a last resort. Credit or credit guarantees would be provided by the financially stronger members to the weaker ones in accordance with predetermined quotas defining both lending obligations and borrowing rights. To the extent that the lending countries are those that have received the most deposits and investments from the oil producers and the borrowers are those that have received the least, this operation will be a form of recycling. Like the IMF facility, the OECD arrangement will take account of the overall financial needs of members and will be conditional upon the avoidance of recourse to restrictive trade measures; however, it will include more stringent conditions relating to energy conservation and development policies. (As a practical matter, however, such conditions can be effective only if the lending countries themselves adopt vigorous policies for energy conservation and development.) Unlike the IMF facility, which receives funds from the oil-exporting nations and, in turn, provides these nations with an internationally guaranteed asset, the OECD arrangement does not involve any direct dealings with the OPEC countries. Thus, these countries will have to take their chances in continuing to lend and invest their surpluses in the financial markets of OECD nations.

The safety-net facility being established by the OECD countries has great merit as a form of financial insurance for a limited period in cases where private and other official recycling falls short of the needs of OECD countries. We particularly endorse the linking of mutual as-

sistance to progress in meeting the shared objectives of lessening dependence on imported oil and maintaining a viable open international trading system. **We recommend whatever authorizing action is required to put a facility such as the safety net into effect promptly.**

Thus far, however, no adequate arrangement has been institutionalized in which OPEC countries would assume a major share of the credit risk of lending to those developing and developed countries hard pressed to meet their oil-import bills. Even with the enlargement of their quotas in IMF and their subscriptions to the World Bank, OPEC countries will be sharing the risk of lending through these institutions only to the extent of the 10 to 15 percent represented by their share of ownership. Although individual OPEC countries have extended credits directly to a number of oil-importing countries, these arrangements have been limited in scale, sporadic, and at terms not always suited to the financial situation of the borrower. **We recommend that the economically strong OECD countries try to work out with the OPEC countries a cooperative arrangement for establishing a new joint fund from which to make loans to those countries that would qualify for aid on the basis of agreed-upon economic criteria. Management of the new institution would be related to contributions and assumption of risk, but the exact proportions of OPEC and OECD contributions and the terms of the loans would be matters for negotiation.** Properly set up, such an arrangement would signify the readiness of OPEC countries to assume responsibility for a fair share of the financial cost and risk involved in dealing with the consequences of their increases in oil prices.

---

* **CEDA** (Australia) believes that the duplication of international financial institutions is unnecessary. Efforts should be made to channel the maximum amount of funds through existing multilateral agencies.

Long-Term Investment of OPEC Surpluses. As banks increasingly respond to the huge flow of so-called petrodollars by accepting such deposits only at reduced rates, pressure is exerted on OPEC countries to diversify their assets. There is already evidence of increased OPEC investment in securities (including equities), in existing real assets such as real estate and businesses, and in the creation or financing of new enterprises.

This trend creates a dilemma for OECD countries. On the one hand, it is clearly desirable to encourage the shift of oil-exporting countries' funds from destabilizing short-term commitments to longer-term, less liquid forms of investment; on the other, a large-scale shift to investment in equities and to the direct purchase of real assets could raise public anxieties about the issue of control because OPEC investments will be not only foreign investments but also foreign government investments.

It is sometimes suggested that in order to attract OPEC investments into long-term bonds, OECD governments should create special issues offering such features as maintenance-of-value guarantees against inflation and devaluation. **We believe there is justification for offering special issues of government securities to OPEC countries in order to provide them with an opportunity to invest very large sums without influencing the market against themselves. But the terms of such special issues should not include guarantees that are not also made available to the general investing public.**

As for OPEC investments in foreign enterprises, we believe these are unlikely to reach a scale that would raise serious question of influence over the national economies of OECD countries. OPEC members regard such commitments as potential hostages in the hands of host governments and therefore will exercise restraint in making them. **Nevertheless, the governments of the OECD countries should take whatever steps are necessary to ensure that full, systematic, and current information is available about foreign investment in their respective countries, including advance consultation in the case of major new official investments; that this information is exchanged and evaluated in OECD; and that intensified efforts are made in OECD to develop guidelines for the treatment of foreign official investments in the light of the new situation, keeping in mind the ultimate objective of securing an open world market for capital.**

Thus far, foreign investment guidelines have been discussed in OECD in terms of national treatment, that is, treatment of private foreign investors equal to that accorded to investors who are nationals of the host country. But national treatment would afford little protection for foreign investment in countries where the government is the principal investor and the role of the private sector is tightly circumscribed. **In the light of the large flow of investments in both directions, consideration should be given to the desirability of substituting the principle of bilateral reci-**

procity for that of national treatment for investments flowing to and from countries in which the government is the principal investor. Under the reciprocity rule, the obligation of the host country would be to treat a foreign investor in a manner equal to that accorded by his home country to a foreign investor. If national treatment were more favorable, it could be applied as a matter of discretion, but it should not be a matter of right.

International Monetary Reform. The vast change in world payments induced by the oil-price increases has interrupted the formal process of reform of the international monetary system. Given present uncertainties, the consensus is that reform should be achieved in an evolutionary manner and that some form of exchange rate flexibility will remain a feature of the international monetary system indefinitely.

The present world payments imbalance has also strengthened the case for a cooperative approach to adjusting and financing the current accounts of oil-importing countries. **It is particularly important under present circumstances to press ahead with the effort to develop and agree upon more effective guidelines for managing floating currencies that would encourage consistent policies among countries and safeguard against exchange-market intervention designed to achieve unjustified competitive advantage.***

PLIGHT OF THE DEVELOPING COUNTRIES

The prospects of the developing countries have changed drastically from those anticipated prior to the oil-price increases late in 1973. The cost of these increases to the developing countries that are not members of OPEC was approximately $10 billion in 1974, an amount equal to the total official development assistance in 1972 from the sixteen member countries of OECD participating in its Development Assistance Committee (DAC). Even the most optimistic earlier projections of capital flows to the developing countries would now be utterly inadequate to sustain satisfactory rates of growth. Half of the developing countries (excluding the People's Republic of China) that are not OPEC members have per capita incomes below $200; their total population is 800 million. For these countries, the previously projected flows of assistance would be insufficient to avoid the appalling prospect of a decline in per capita incomes.

See memorandum by *FRAZAR B. WILDE, page 93.

The impact that the increased costs of petroleum imports have had on the developing countries cannot be viewed in isolation. Related factors have caused lesser but still substantial increases in the costs of imported food, fertilizer, machinery and equipment, and other developmental goods. At the same time, economic stagnation in the industrial countries is adversely affecting exports from the developing countries and therefore their capacity to import.

The World Bank has estimated the concessionary aid that would be required to achieve minimum acceptable growth rates, defined as 4 percent continuing growth in per capita GNP for developing countries with per capita incomes over $200 and 2 percent for those with per capita incomes under $200. To achieve these results, concessionary aid would have to rise from $12 billion in 1973 to $30 billion in 1980. In addition, borrowing by developing countries on market terms would have to rise from approximately $9 billion in 1973 to $24 billion in 1980. A substantial portion of these increases in net capital flows will simply offset the higher prices of goods and services imported by the developing countries.

Finance at Market Terms. There is a reasonable chance that many of the middle- and higher-income developing countries can meet their needs for funds at market terms by borrowing from existing sources.

Twenty-eight developing countries that are not OPEC members resorted to Eurocurrency borrowing in 1974, mostly on terms from seven to ten years and at floating interest rates. If the central banks of developed countries stand behind the Eurocurrency banks as lenders of last resort, this market should continue to play a role (although a more limited one) in recycling oil surpluses to the more creditworthy developing countries. However, the principal intermediaries for recycling to this group of countries will be IMF and the World Bank.

With its expanded oil facility and enlarged normal drawing facilities as a result of increased quotas, IMF will be a prime source of medium-term credits to enable developing countries to meet their current account deficits over the critical period to 1980. The World Bank should become an important intermediary in recycling oil money at long term, especially to developing countries that do not have the standing to borrow directly in private financial markets but that are nevertheless in a position to assume additional debt-service obligations under the conditions established for the bank's hard-loan window. In order to finance these operations, the bank has borrowed large sums directly from the oil-exporting countries. **We recommend that the World Bank also be enabled to mobilize oil revenues indirectly by being granted ready access to OECD capital markets.**

Concessionary Aid. * Much more difficult than meeting the requirements of developing countries for finance on market terms is the provision of adequate amounts of soft money to meet the desperate needs of the poorest and least creditworthy developing countries. Some OPEC countries have made a substantial start in committing funds to this group, mostly through bilateral arrangements. The terms and conditions of these commitments have not always been made generally known, however, nor is it always clear whether they are intended to be one-time or continuing operations. In addition to grants and low-interest loans, assistance from OPEC members could, to a greater extent than in the past, take the form of lower prices for oil sold to the poorest developing countries or of repayment in local currency.

We have already noted our approval of the new interest-subsidy arrangement of the IMF oil facility, which will make it possible for the fund to extend medium-term credit on concessionary terms to the poorest developing countries. **The interest-subsidy technique will also be used to enable the World Bank to establish a "third window" for making long-term loans at rates in between those charged for the bank's hard loans and those charged for the very soft loans of its International Development Association (IDA). We recommend that our governments contribute the sums necessary to enable such a "third window" to operate on a modest initial scale as a means of increasing the World Bank's flexibility in assisting developing countries that require concessionary finance.**

However, we see IDA playing the central role in helping the poorest and least creditworthy developing countries. The terms of IDA credits amount to grants for 75 percent of their face value even without taking the inflationary erosion of the principal into account. **We urge contributions to the International Development Association by the member governments of both OPEC and OECD in amounts sufficient to enable the poorest countries to sustain acceptable rates of growth.**

Whatever form concessionary lending takes, a key question is how the total amount of necessary concessionary lending should be shared by OPEC and OECD countries. We therefore propose what might be a

See memorandum by *G. BARRON MALLORY, page 93.

reasonable basis for dealing with the foreign exchange gap of developing countries requiring concessionary assistance. Those OPEC countries with higher per capita incomes might contribute concessionary aid in amounts related to the additional price of petroleum paid by other developing countries; OECD countries might be asked to increase their flows of grants and soft loans in amounts related to the increased costs paid by the developing countries for imports of other goods and services.

INTERNATIONAL TRADE POLICY

Among the important international economic questions precipitated by the energy crisis are several issues of trade policy.

Trade Measures for Balance-of-Payments Adjustment. What role should trade measures such as quantitative restrictions, import surcharges, and export subsidies play in balance-of-payments adjustment, and what type of international constraints should be placed on their use? These issues have come to the fore because of the unprecedented change in the structure of world payments and in particular because of the deterioration of the current accounts of most OECD countries, resulting from the increase in oil prices.

Under the existing system of flexible exchange rates, the case for the use of trade measures in adjusting balance-of-payments deficits is diminished because changes in rates can more readily be allowed to carry the burden of adjustment. But countries may still prefer trade measures because of the time required for an exchange rate change to affect the flow of trade and because under certain circumstances currency depreciation may be more inflationary.

The General Agreement on Tariffs and Trade (GATT) and the IMF Articles of Agreement should be amended to permit countries in balance-of-payments difficulties to use appropriate trade measures in addition to quotas, but any such measure should be subject to more stringent IMF surveillance of its justification on balance-of-payments grounds. At the same time, GATT would retain jurisdiction over the acceptability of the restriction in terms of commercial policy (e.g., compliance with the rule of nondiscrimination, avoidance of unnecessary damage to the trading partners, and allowing the importation of commercial samples). **

See memorandum by *HERMAN L. WEISS, page 94.

✳ **KEIZAI DOYUKAI** (Japan) dissents from this recommendation. Such amendments to GATT articles as are suggested here will require revisions not only of Article XII dealing with quantitative import restrictions but also of many other articles. This will inevitably present some complex problems that will have far-reaching impacts on the international trade system. Furthermore, Keizai Doyukai believes that IMF articles should not be revised before we have a more stable climate in the world economy.

New International Rules on Export Controls. The oil embargo in the winter of 1973–1974 dramatized a major gap in the system of multilateral rules governing international trade policy. Until recently, trade policy concentrated on improving access to markets through the reduction or elimination of import restrictions, but it paid little attention to ensuring access to supplies by limiting the possibility of imposing restraints on exports.

There is wide support for more effective GATT rules to deal with export restrictions in situations of short supply. **In the new round of trade negotiations, every effort should be made to establish clearly defined provisions on export restrictions. The main objectives should be to ensure international consultation before export restrictions are used to meet shortage situations, to define permissible measures restricting exports, to give effect to the principle of equitable sharing, and to encourage the development of positive and constructive export programs rather than restrictive measures to cope with shortages over the longer term.**

Politically Motivated Export Restrictions. At the present time, there are no effective international constraints on politically motivated trade restrictions such as the oil embargo in late 1973 and early 1974, the OECD strategic-trade controls, and the U.S. embargo on exports to Cuba.

Although export restrictions are outlawed under GATT, the rule is subject to a variety of exceptions, the most sweeping of which is the national security article. But with the exception of Kuwait, the main countries that participated in the oil embargo are not now parties to GATT (although membership may become more attractive to them as they become industrialized). However, there is a serious question whether it would be possible within the framework of GATT or other forums to negotiate a tighter national security provision that would effectively limit embargoes and other forms of politically motivated export restrictions.

Producer Cartels and Commodity Agreements. Export arrangements may be designed to influence world market prices through either a producer cartel (such as OPEC) or an international commodity agreement (such as the tin agreement) in which both producers and consumers participate.

Under GATT, intergovernmental arrangements on commodities involving restrictions on trade are sanctioned only if they conform to the criterion of equitable representation of consuming and producing countries in the negotiation and administration of the agreement. Trade restriction agreements that represent producers only are therefore a violation of GATT. **We believe that multilateral arrangements on certain internationally traded commodities consistent with the GATT criterion of equitable representation may serve a useful purpose in moderating sharp fluctuations in the prices of primary products and in preventing arbitrary interruptions of supply. A more positive attitude toward such arrangements on the part of the OECD governments might help to deter the present tendency toward the formation of producer cartels.***

An international commodity agreement involving the principal exporters and importers of petroleum would be an alternative to the OPEC approach to control of the world oil market. Such an agreement would involve formidable negotiating problems, both between exporters and importers and within each group, in reaching decisions on a price range, export quotas, benefits for new exporters, and enforcement mechanisms. In addition to the technical difficulties, the negotiators would have to contend with mutual suspicions and different assessments of bargaining leverage.

When the atmosphere improves, however, the advantages of a cooperative multilateral approach may prove sufficiently appealing to make it a feasible way of ordering world trade in petroleum. It may then be possible to negotiate a mutually beneficial commodity agreement on oil that would include provisions on price, supply, or other factors. Such an arrangement would need to be flexible enough to allow price adjustments as market conditions change. It should be recognized, however, that difficult theoretical and practical problems are involved in determining the long-run supply price for exhaustible resources. **We do not regard**

See memorandum by *HERMAN L. WEISS, page 94.

indexing—that is, a system of linking the price of oil to the price of other goods—as an appropriate principle for setting the price of oil or other commodities because it would stimulate inflation and rigidify prices on a basis that is unrelated to market conditions, including long-term trends in technology.*

 IDEP (France) believes that the rejection of indexing should be seen against a background in which each country (producer or consumer) is struggling to control inflation and all feel themselves to be allied in this effort and are taking similar actions, although with due allowance for their respective situations.

Processing Oil and Other Raw Materials in Producing Countries. Developing countries that export raw materials have increasingly sought to process their resources locally for supply to the world market. In the case of oil, some producing countries have ambitious plans to develop not only substantial local refining but also national petrochemical industries based on domestically produced oil and gas.

Local processing is viewed by most producing countries as a natural path to development. In addition to augmenting foreign exchange earnings, it increases employment, provides opportunities to upgrade the skills of the work force, and stimulates ancillary industrial activities.

As new capacity for processing raw materials is needed, local processing in developing countries should be encouraged as a legitimate part of a strategy of development. This encouragement should be subject to the economic feasibility of specific projects and consistent with the need to ensure stable supplies of processed products. We recommend that in the forthcoming trade negotiations a special effort be made to reduce the degree of tariff discrimination against imports of processed products. In the case of strategic materials, such liberalization should be subject to adequate safeguards in forms such as stockpiles of processed products in the importing countries and adequate reserve capacity for processing.

COOPERATION AMONG THE INDUSTRIAL COUNTRIES*

Most of the measures discussed in this statement are intended to deal with the short- and medium-term economic and financial consequences of the increased price of oil. Taken alone, however, they are insufficient to reduce the vulnerability of the industrial countries to further increases in the price of oil and to interruptions in its supply.

Some governments have attempted to protect themselves by entering into bilateral arrangements with oil producers. Although this is an understandable reaction on the part of resource-poor countries to the first phase of the oil crisis, such a go-it-alone strategy carries the danger of bidding up prices and stabilizing them at a higher level. But when such bilateral deals are made, we see a role for OECD or some other appropriate organization in improving the bargaining position of its members in obtaining oil on more favorable terms. If information on bilateral arrangements is pooled, the chances that any importing country will act with inadequate knowledge of market conditions will be reduced. And by subjecting bilateral deals to guidelines and mutual discussion among member countries, OECD could exercise some restraint on arrangements that bid up prices unnecessarily or tie up supplies or markets excessively.

The best long-run solution, however, lies in cooperation among the industrial countries to establish contingency plans for emergencies, to conserve energy use, and to develop new and diversified sources of energy both at home and abroad.

Cooperation in Emergencies. All countries must protect themselves against possible interruptions in the supply of oil. Some are better equipped for this than others because they are less dependent on imported oil. But national economies are so interdependent that no country can ignore the economic welfare of its principal trading partners. Countries with more abundant oil supplies should be prepared to share them with others. Countries with less abundant supplies must in turn assume part of the burden of emergency preparedness by maintaining large stockpiles and conserving energy during any emergency. An international agreement is thus essential.

Although no ideal basis for an agreement exists, the eighteen-nation emergency oil-storage and -sharing program of the new International Energy Agency (IEA) represents a reasonable and workable compromise. **We welcome the agreement on emergency oil storage and sharing**

See memorandum by *HERMAN L. WEISS, page 94.

among the countries in the International Energy Agency and urge its early ratification or approval by the signatory governments. Its ten-year life and the virtually automatic character of its provisions mean that the program will contribute much as an antidote for and deterrent to any oil-supply interruption. However, the agreement would be strengthened if all OECD nations were to subscribe to it.

Energy Conservation. An important element of the IEA program is the energy-conservation requirements it imposes on members in the event of an emergency. **To make the International Energy Agency program effective, each nation must maintain a continuously updated standby plan for emergency conservation and fuel allocation.** Indeed, with or without emergencies, slowing the growth of energy consumption is desirable as a means of putting downward pressure on oil prices, improving the payments positions of oil-importing countries, strengthening their ability to withstand supply interruptions, and encouraging a more efficient pattern of energy utilization. Moreover, energy conservation also serves the interests of those oil producers that want to avoid depleting their oil wealth before they have become industrialized.

Effective conservation will, however, be difficult to achieve. Economic structures and personal life-styles will have to change. Conservation will be mainly a matter for national (rather than international) action. *OECD countries should give higher priority to the development of comprehensive national conservation plans to restrain their own oil consumption and imports by whatever means are appropriate to their economies.*

Of course, different countries have different capacities for conservation. An informal international understanding is essential to avoid a situation in which energy-conserving nations simply release supplies to nonconserving nations. IEA might attempt to establish nonbinding but indicative energy-consumption targets for each of its members. Not enough is known about different countries' experiences in conservation or about conservation technologies in general. **We recommend that the International Energy Agency establish an international clearing system for information on techniques and economic policies for energy conservation and both establish and coordinate the most wide-ranging international program of conservation research possible.***

New Sources of Supply. Although conservation may help to achieve independence from uncertain sources of supply, conservation alone can-

See memorandum by *JOHN SAGAN, page 95.

not possibly ensure it. New sources of energy must be developed. Few countries have the capacity to be totally self-sufficient, but international cooperation in the development of new energy supplies can help to diminish present dependence on oil imports.

Cooperation is particularly desirable to ensure adequate supplies of enriched uranium and to conduct urgently needed research.* We welcome IEA's inclusion of these matters within its mandate and suggest that particular research areas ripe for international cooperation in this or another suitable forum include improved techniques for coal mining, reclamation of surface-mined land, cleaner burning of coal in power stations, and economically feasible coal gasification and liquefaction. For the longer term, there should be the most extensive international cooperation in research on solar energy, the extraction of energy from refuse, geothermal energy, and nuclear fusion.*

Investors in energy development are faced with a potentially serious problem. Can they be sure that their investment will be profitable if, particularly as a result of their own contributions to an increased world energy supply, oil prices should fall in the future? *What is needed is some form of national guarantee to investors in expensive new energy sources. The guarantee should be primarily directed to investment in high-cost unconventional fuels such as synthetics and shale. In particular cases, special incentives may also be needed for investment in conventional fuels. However, we see no present need for a common floor price for petroleum; in fact, we believe it could even strengthen OPEC's ability to keep prices up. The nature of the guarantee for high-cost energy investment is a matter of national policy, and we tend to favor a case-by-case approach.**

The cooperation required to meet emergencies, to conserve energy, and to develop new sources will not be easy to achieve. Many of the measures we have advocated will be expensive, but they are essential for the future prosperity of the industrial world. Furthermore, the collaboration needed among consuming countries could provide the basis for wider cooperation with the producing countries in advancing their industrialization and assisting the poorest developing countries.

See memoranda by *ELVIS J. STAHR, page 95.

Chapter 2

Domestic
Economic Implications

THE RISE IN THE PRICE OF OIL has had very different effects on the individual industrial countries, according to their degree of dependence on imported oil and the state of their balance of payments, especially on current account. Nevertheless, some general points can be made about the domestic economic implications of the oil-price increases.

INFLATION AND LIVING STANDARDS

As a result of the action of OPEC members, consumers have to pay higher prices not only for petroleum but also for other forms of energy. The rise in the price of oil imported into the OECD area in 1973 and 1974 amounted directly to about 2 percent of the importers' GNP. When the effect of higher oil prices on the prices of other forms of energy is taken into account, the impact on the overall OECD price level has been estimated at almost 3½ percent of GNP. (See Figure 2.) Thus, approximately half the acceleration of OECD's consumer price increase during 1974 (to nearly 15 percent, compared with 8 percent in 1973) may be attributed to higher energy prices.*

 IDEP (France) understands this to mean that increases in oil prices at the end of 1973 and in 1974 had their full inflationary impact in 1974.

However, the full impact of the rise in oil prices was higher than these figures indicate. Increased prices for a product as basic as petroleum not only led to higher prices for goods produced by energy-using industries but also stimulated workers' demands for wage increases to keep up with the rising prices. By giving new impetus to the wage-price spiral, therefore, the oil-price rise also contributed to inflation indirectly.

The rise in oil prices and their maintenance at current levels in real terms implies a deterioration in the terms of trade of oil importers and a consequent loss of real income compared with the situation prior to 1974. The extent of the loss depends upon the degree to which the financial transfers to the OPEC countries are matched by corresponding real transfers of goods and services. If the oil producers were to spend the entire increase (amounting to about $70 billion for OECD countries) on current imports, the transfer would be equal to approximately 2 percent of the GNP of the OECD countries. This is by no means an inconsiderable sum. Although it may not amount to more than one-half of the normal growth of OECD output in a single year prior to 1974, the $70 billion would be transferred every year.

However, the full impact on real incomes will not be felt for some time because of the limited ability of OPEC countries to increase their imports in the short run. To the extent that their increased oil income is invested abroad rather than spent for current imports, the real burden of the transfer is shifted to the future. Later, as the members of OPEC develop and diversify their economies, the mix will shift to larger current transfers of wealth and diminished mortgaging of future OECD output.

Whatever the time profile of the transfer of goods and services, a loss in real income has occurred for each importing country as a whole. To the extent that particular groups avoid sharing this loss, they pass the burden on to other groups and contribute to the inflationary spiral. *Among the urgent tasks facing the governments of importing countries is that of educating their people about the true dimensions and implications of the energy problem and the consequent need for restraint in demands for income adjustments.*

OUTPUT AND EMPLOYMENT

Output and employment in the industrial countries are affected by two types of adjustment to higher oil prices: structural changes in the composition of output that correspond to altered patterns of consumption

FIGURE 2: RISE IN ENERGY BILL[a] AS PERCENT OF TOTAL DOMESTIC EXPENDITURE, 1973 AND 1974

	Total, 1973 and 1974	Oil as Percent of Total
CANADA	2.3	1.7
UNITED STATES	2.2	1.4
JAPAN	4.3	3.3
AUSTRALIA AND NEW ZEALAND	3.4	2.3
FRANCE	3.6	2.9
GERMANY	3.1	1.9
ITALY	5.9	5.3
UNITED KINGDOM	5.5	3.9
NORTHERN EUROPE[b]	3.9	3.0
SOUTHERN EUROPE[c]	4.3	3.8
TOTAL OECD[d]	3.3	2.3[e]
OECD EUROPE	4.1	3.0

[a] Figures are for oil, hard coal, and natural gas and include import prices and domestic producer prices; wholesale and retail markups are not included. Figures exclude hydroelectricity and nuclear power.

[b] Austria, Belgium-Luxembourg, Denmark, Finland, Ireland, Norway, Sweden, and Switzerland.

[c] Greece, Portugal, Spain, and Turkey.

[d] Based on 1973 GNP weights.

[e] Includes 1.8 percent for oil imports from outside OECD.

SOURCE: *OECD Observer* 74 (March–April 1975).

and of investment and the overall deflationary consequences of the reduction in domestic consumption in real terms.

The structural problem involves changes in the pattern of consumer spending, such as the shifts from automobiles to mass transit and from large to small cars. Other adaptations to higher relative oil prices involve redesigning industrial processes to conserve fuel and to shift to cheaper forms of energy. These changes are obviously desirable and should be encouraged by appropriate public policies.

The second problem is basically one of economic stabilization. How can full employment be maintained in the face of the deflationary consequences of a decline in consumer spending in real terms? It is useful to think of the oil-price increase as an excise tax imposed on the consumption of oil. The demand for oil is relatively inelastic with respect to price in the short run; therefore, consumers will spend a larger percentage of their income on petroleum products, which will leave them less for other things. This absorption of purchasing power by the petroleum tax, the proceeds of which accrue to OPEC governments, will reduce effective demand in the importing countries relative to their capacity to produce goods and services. The result will be a tendency for domestic output and employment to fall.

Some of this deflationary pressure will be offset by increased imports by OPEC countries from the rest of the world. But, as we have already indicated, approximately $60 billion of the proceeds of the high oil prices remained surplus to OPEC needs for current imports in 1974. This figure provides a rough indication of the initial deflationary effect.[1] To the extent that the surplus oil revenues are used to increase real investment in the OECD countries, and to the extent that consumers in importing countries attempt to maintain their living standards in the face of the petroleum tax by reducing their savings, the downward pressure on employment and output will be offset. On balance, however, we would not expect a major automatic offset from these sources.

---

[1] An unpublished econometric study of the impact of the oil crisis on the growth of GNP in the developed countries has been made by Professor Jean Waelbroeck of the Free University of Brussels. Using a model that links the economies of different countries, Waelbroeck applies dynamic multipliers to estimate not only the direct effect on each country but also the indirect effects resulting from the deterioration of each country's exports. He concludes that the downward impact of the oil crisis on GNP (1.4 percent in 1974 and 2.5 percent in 1976) is considerable and that it constitutes a major cause of the current recession.

Although experience varies widely by country, the deflationary impact of higher oil prices accentuated a sharp cyclical downturn in 1974 for the OECD countries as a group; total production actually declined slightly from the 1973 level. Yet, the capacity of the importing countries to absorb the burden of higher oil prices depends in the first instance on the health and vitality of their own economies. *Clearly, one of the first tasks of the governments of the OECD countries is to counter domestic economic stagnation, which has been exacerbated by oil-price increases and which has resulted in tremendous human suffering and waste of resources.*

The precise mix of policies for stimulating the domestic economy and combating inflation must necessarily be adapted to the economic and political circumstances of individual countries. In an interdependent world, however, domestic economic stimulation results in an increase in imports and therefore adversely affects the balance of payments on current account at a time when many industrial countries are already running huge deficits. Appropriate expansionary policies must be pursued simultaneously by trading partners (also experiencing slow growth or stagnation) so that import demand and export opportunities rise together; otherwise, there is a danger that government fiscal and monetary stimuli will be too hesitant and inadequate in scale. It is important to make provision for the closest consultation with respect to stabilization policies among the industrialized countries.

In designing expansionary fiscal and monetary policies to offset the depressing impact of oil-price increases, countries have a choice of stimulating either consumption or investment or both. A substantial stimulus is clearly required both to consumption and to investment during the current recession. However, encouraging consumption will contribute little to the ability of oil-importing countries to finance the real burden of higher energy costs in the long run. **As OECD countries move closer to full employment, therefore, we recommend that government policies lean toward greater stimulus to investment (e.g., through more liberal depreciation allowances and investment credits).** Ultimately, the OECD countries will be aided in paying off their growing debt to the members of OPEC by increased output from new productive capacity, or they will be able to reduce the growth of that debt by investing in other sources of energy, thereby achieving greater independence from uncertain sources of supplies.

Chapter 3

International Financial Issues

OIL-IMPORTING COUNTRIES should take whatever steps they can to reduce their combined current account deficit by conserving energy and developing alternative supplies. However, such measures are likely to yield substantial results only gradually. In the short run, importing countries have no option but to accept a large deterioration (from the 1973 base) in their combined current account matched by corresponding inflows of capital from the oil exporters.

What, then, are the international financial policy problems caused by the new situation? Basically, they derive from the fact that the automatic matching of payments and receipts for the oil importers as a group will not occur automatically for each of them individually. How individual countries resolve the balance-of-payments problem is of crucial importance to the functioning of the international economic system. In this chapter, we explore three aspects of the problem: how the current account deficits of the oil importers should be distributed, how a smooth recycling of surplus oil revenues corresponding to the pattern of current account deficits of individual countries can be ensured, and how the new situation will affect international monetary reform.

BALANCE-OF-PAYMENTS ADJUSTMENT

Individual importing countries may seek to minimize their own particular deficits. For some countries (e.g., Italy and the United Kingdom), the deterioration in the current account is superimposed on existing deficits. Whatever their cause, large current account deficits tend to constrain economic policy. For example, countries may be loath to adopt expansionary measures in the face of high unemployment because of the effect of such measures on the current account. This is particularly true if the capital inflow that finances the current account is viewed as unstable.

Because of the limited ability of oil exporters to increase their imports in the short run, an oil-importing country can reduce its own deficit only by increasing the deficits of the other oil-importing countries. The standard methods for reducing a deficit are to restrain aggregate demand, restrict imports or subsidize exports, and depreciate the exchange rate. If such policies were generally followed, the inevitable net result would be a mutually destructive contraction of both internal demand and world trade.

How, then, should the total current deficit of the importing countries be distributed? No fully satisfactory formula for resolving this thorny problem has yet emerged. It is sometimes suggested that countries should attempt to balance their current account receipts and expenditures exclusive of the deficits resulting from the increase in the price of oil. This would mean that although individual deficits and surpluses unrelated to the oil-price increases would be corrected, the increase in each country's oil-related deficit would be accepted and an effort would be made to finance it through capital flows.

Although useful as a general guideline in the short term, this approach is subject to varying interpretation. According to the most narrow view, a country could take into account only changes in the net value of trade in oil. Or it could also include net changes in other current transactions with the oil-exporting countries. A broader interpretation would take into account the shift in international competitiveness of national industries with varying degrees of dependence on energy imports or even the differential overall effects of the oil-price increases on national rates of inflation.

As a practical approach to the problem of balance-of-payments adjustment for the OECD countries, we recommend that each country accept its narrowly defined oil-induced current deficit in the short run (say, 1975 and 1976) and attempt to finance this deficit through private and official capital flows from abroad. Deficits not directly related to oil-price increases should, of course, be corrected promptly. After 1976, as the long-term investment of OPEC surpluses settles into more stable patterns, we would suggest a gradual shift to greater reliance on correction of the remaining deficits on current account plus long-term capital accounts through exchange rate adjustments.

EUROCURRENCY MARKET

The Eurocurrency market is an international pool of bank deposits denominated in foreign currencies that are held in European commercial banks, including European branches of American banks. These bank deposits, denominated in dollars, pounds, marks, French francs, and other convertible currencies (but excluding bank deposits of their own currencies), constitute the funds for the Eurocurrency market. Until recently, most of the Eurocurrency deposits were in U.S. dollars, giving rise to the term *Eurodollars*. The dollar is still the predominant currency, accounting for over 70 percent of the total funds.

Eurocurrency deposits arise, for instance, when an owner of a demand deposit at a U.S. bank (or an Arab sheik who received dollar proceeds from sales of oil) transfers his account to a European bank (or a branch office of a U.S. bank) in exchange for a claim payable in dollars against that European bank. The European bank (*Eurobank*) that receives this Eurodollar deposit may then lend the dollars to another bank in Europe, to a corporation, or to an individual.

London is the center of the Eurocurrency market. In 1974, U.K. banks accounted for more than half of the total Eurocurrency holdings reported by banks in eight major European countries. Not surprisingly, the most important factors behind the growth of the Eurocurrency market in 1974 were the higher price of oil and rising revenues of OPEC. The massive inflow of oil revenues sharply boosted both the supply of Eurocurrency funds and the demand for them.

The Eurocurrency market comprises short-term as well as medium- and long-term bank credits. In addition, however, there is the Eurobond market, in which funds are raised by the issue of medium- and long-term securities. The Eurofinancial system includes this entire complex of financial operations.

However, there is great need for close and frequent consultation among the financial officials of the principal trading nations with a view to agreeing on consistent balance-of-payments objectives. These consultations must take into account the internal economic conditions, the balance-of-payments impact of higher oil prices, and the ability to attract foreign capital on market terms in the case of each country.

OECD and IMF are the appropriate forums for the kind of consultation envisaged here because they have an established record of concern for the consistency of the balance-of-payments aims and policies of their member countries. We believe that the present strains on the international financial system make such cooperation more urgent than ever.

RECYCLING OF FINANCIAL SURPLUSES
OF OIL EXPORTERS

The basic problem of recycling is to ensure that the pattern of capital flows matches the internationally accepted distribution of current account deficits among oil-consuming countries. To the extent that OPEC countries invest directly in oil-importing countries in proportion to their current account deficits, the need to recycle is minimized. This is the simplest solution in terms of the mechanics of the international financial system; it is also the most desirable in principle because the OPEC countries, which brought on the world payments imbalance by quadrupling the price of oil, would be the ones to bear the ultimate credit risk involved in helping weak nations to pay their higher oil-import bills.

To the extent that the initial flows of capital from the oil exporters go disproportionately to economically strong countries and insufficiently to weak ones, secondary flows of capital among oil-consuming countries are needed. This process creates major technical strains on the international financial system. More fundamentally, it is a way of shifting onto others the risk of lending to weak countries to finance the increased costs of OPEC oil.

Little official information is available from the OPEC countries themselves on where their balance-of-payments surpluses are being invested. Therefore, estimates are based largely on information compiled by the receiving countries and on reports of individual transactions. The U.S. Department of the Treasury has compiled a breakdown of how the OPEC countries deployed their surplus in 1974 (see Figure 3).

FIGURE 3: HOW OPEC COUNTRIES INVESTED THEIR SURPLUS IN 1974

	Amount (billions)	Percent of Total Investment
EUROCURRENCY MARKET *Basically in bank deposits*	$22.50	37.5
UNITED STATES *Roughly $6 billion in short- and longer-term U.S. government securities; some $4 billion in bank deposits, bankers' acceptances, and other money-market paper; less than $1 billion in property and equities*	11.25	18.8
UNITED KINGDOM *Assets denominated in sterling, including U.K. government securities, bank deposits, other money-market instruments, property, and equities[a]*	7.50	12.5
OTHER DEVELOPED COUNTRIES *Mostly direct lending by OPEC countries to official and quasi-official institutions in other European countries and Japan*	5.50	9.2

a Amount is additional to large Eurocurrency deposits in London banks.

As Figure 3 shows, in 1974, about two-thirds of the surplus revenues flowed into liquid investments in the Eurocurrency market and the traditional national money markets of New York and London. Operating as intermediaries, these institutions have served as the main vehicles for recycling oil money to countries that need it to cover their deficits. The efficiency of market forces in accomplishing this intermediation has been greatly strengthened by the termination of U.S. controls on capital outflows and by the easing of restrictions on capital inflows on the part of a number of European countries.

However, because the sums involved are so large, the ability of capital markets to accommodate them without severe dislocations has

	Amount (billions)	Percent of Total Investment
INTERNATIONAL INSTITUTIONS	$ 3.50	5.8
Obligations of such institutions as the World Bank and IMF		
DEVELOPING COUNTRIES AND OPEC LENDING INSTITUTIONS	4.00	6.6
Funds transferred directly from OPEC countries to other developing countries; funds channeled to various OPEC lending institutions such as the Kuwait Fund and the Arab Bank for Africa		
REMAINDER	5.75	9.6
Only limited information available; presumably includes funds directed to investment management accounts, private-sector loans, and purchases of corporate securities in Europe and Japan		
TOTAL	**$60.00**	100.0

become a matter of international concern. It may be well, therefore, to begin by comparing this volume with some measure of the size of the markets that have to absorb them. The volume of funds raised by non-financial sectors in U.S. credit markets is now about $200 billion a year. For all industrial countries together, the total has been estimated at two to three times that amount, or seven to ten times the volume of funds likely to flow from the oil producers. Over time, the size of national credit markets will increase, and the flow of surplus oil revenue will diminish as the capacity of the exporting countries to absorb imported goods and services grows.

A large part of the oil revenues, however, is being invested in the

Eurocurrency market rather than in national money markets. The Euro-currency market has grown rapidly in recent years. According to the Bank for International Settlements, the net size of this market (after eliminating claims of one bank on another) grew by $40 billion in 1973 and by $45 billion in 1974, bringing the total to $177 billion by the end of 1974. As these figures clearly demonstrate, the flow into the Euro-currency market of a substantial portion of OPEC's $60 billion surplus would constitute a very large element of total net flows and could strain the facilities of this market. Evidence of strain is already apparent in the steep decline in Eurocurrency bank credits from $19 billion in the first half of 1974 to $8 billion in the second half.

Given the magnitude of the oil surpluses, the process of recycling them has raised problems for financial markets and institutions that cannot be ignored. OPEC funds are coming into the markets as very short term deposits, but the banks have to extend credit to consuming countries at long term. Although borrowing short and lending long is the traditional function of bankers, the risks may become unacceptable when the sums involved are so large and the deposits are held by only a few foreign governments.

In thinking about this gap in maturities, however, a distinction must be drawn between the form of oil exporters' deposits, which may be short term, and their effective maturity, which is likely to be long term. So long as OPEC countries are not in a position to redeem their financial claims by developing an import surplus (a process that for some will take many years), their funds will continue to remain on deposit, although switching from one short-term asset to another or into longer-term assets may take place. Similarly, there is no possibility for the borrowing countries as a group to liquidate their debts until they develop an export surplus with the oil producers. Whatever the form of the lending and borrowing, therefore, the effective term of these transactions must match the time phasing of the current account of the balance of payments of both the oil exporters and the oil importers.

Although true in general, none of this answers the individual banker worried about a declining capital ratio or large shifts of liquid liabilities out of his bank while holding assets of long maturity. One reason for such shifts may be the desire of holders of liquid funds to switch to other currencies. Under the present flexible exchange rate system, such movements can help to bring about desirable exchange rate adjustments. But they can also be disruptive, contributing either to payments imbalances or to excessive rate changes. Such destabilizing shifts of oil producers' funds need not reflect any intention to rock the boat; indeed, the presumption is that holders of large assets have a major stake in international monetary stability. But asset preferences can change quickly, and the possibility of abrupt switches, including switches out of specific currencies for political reasons, cannot be ruled out.

However, the risk of destabilizing shifts in funds is reduced to the extent that the market encourages the desired change in the structure of maturities by adjusting the spread between short- and long-term rates on both the lending and the deposit sides. Banks have been reducing the interest paid on short-term deposits as compared with the rate charged on longer-term loans. As more banks make these adjustments, financial markets will tend toward equilibrium.

Nevertheless, some banks, particularly in the Eurocurrency markets, may find themselves in a liquidity squeeze. Liquidity problems should be distinguished from solvency problems. A liquidity problem can arise through no fault of the bank because of depositor withdrawals; a solvency problem implies poor lending and management decisions. In the case of Eurobank liquidity problems, the home office of the bank should be able to turn to its central bank as a lender of last resort. (The technical problem of defining the home office of a consortium bank should be resolved by negotiation.) **We strongly endorse the joint policy announced by the monetary authorities of the principal industrial countries that "means are available . . . and will be used if and when necessary" to help banks in the Eurocurrency system that get into trouble through a sudden shift of funds.**[1]

In time, an increasing proportion of OPEC funds may be attracted into less liquid investments (e.g., equities, direct investment, real estate, and special government issues). Special government issues have already attracted substantial amounts of OPEC money because they permit the investor to transact very large sums without influencing the market against himself.

Whether short or long term, however, the assets favored by OPEC investors are those based in the countries with the strongest economies and the broadest markets. Similarly, the banks that receive Eurocurrency deposits from OPEC prefer to lend them to governments and private borrowers in countries with modest debt burdens and more favorable

---

[1] Bank for International Settlements, press review (Basel: September 10, 1974).

payments prospects. The problem therefore is to recycle OPEC funds among oil-consuming countries so that those in a weaker position are enabled to finance their essential petroleum imports. To the extent that the capital markets do not accomplish this automatically, special government initiatives or new international facilities are required. (The particular problems of developing countries are treated in Chapter 4.)

On the bilateral level, the West German government's 1974 loan to Italy, backed by a portion of Italy's gold reserve, is an example of international cooperation to meet the problem. Another official bilateral facility is a swap arrangement between central banks; this could be used to bridge a period in which direct financing of oil deficits was being arranged. Consideration should also be given to enlarging existing swap facilities so that, through rollovers, they can play a more direct part in financing oil deficits while remaining adequate to deal with the shorter-term reversible payments movements for which they were originally intended.

On the multilateral level, the countries of the European Economic Community (the Common Market) have agreed on a plan under which they could jointly borrow up to $3 billion from oil-producing countries to help members cover balance-of-payments deficits caused by oil imports. The loans will be jointly guaranteed by the nine European governments. They will be made on a case-by-case basis by the finance ministers of the Common Market and will have a minimum term of five years.

Such modest initiatives are to be welcomed, but the dimensions of the problem require much larger scale and more universally applicable international recycling arrangements. In considering broader facilities, several guidelines are applicable. First, insofar as OECD countries assume the ultimate credit risk for loans or guarantees to each other, these countries should be in a position to set their own terms and conditions for such assistance rather than be subject to conditions laid down in organizations with wider membership. Second, special finance on an adequate scale should be provided for the developing countries, especially those most severely affected, primarily through an expansion in the operations of existing multilateral institutions, especially IMF and the World Bank, in which they are full participants. Third, OPEC and OECD countries have an interest in a healthy world economy; therefore, they should equitably share the risk of lending to countries in weak financial positions.

In recent months, considerable progress has been achieved in putting these principles into practice. The IMF oil facility, which was established on a scale of about $4 billion for 1974, was renewed in 1975 for more than $6 billion. It was designed to assist oil-importing countries during 1974 and 1975 with the funds needed to maintain essential imports without resorting to undesirable policies. Drawings from the IMF facility may be outstanding for up to seven years, with repayment beginning after the third year. Because the adjustment is more difficult under the present circumstances, the average term of five years is somewhat longer than the fund's normal lending period. Access to the new facility depends mainly on the increase in the total cost of a member's oil imports, its quota in the fund, and the size of its monetary reserves.

The bulk of the resources for the new facility is borrowed from the oil-exporting countries. Loans to the oil facility are denominated in Special Drawing Rights and therefore are protected against the risk of fluctuations in the exchange value of individual currencies. Claims under the loans are also liquid because of a provision entitling countries to repayment in case of balance-of-payments difficulty. Because of the liquidity and security of lending to IMF, the interest rate of 7¼ percent for 1975 is below that prevailing in national capital markets. Interest charged to borrowers depends on the maturity of the loans but will average around 7¾ percent under the oil facility for 1975.

Italy has been the largest single borrower, but a sizable portion of the oil facility's funds is being lent to developing countries. Of special benefit to the approximately thirty poorest developing countries is an interest subsidy introduced in 1975 on the $1.3 to $1.7 billion that IMF estimates they will receive from the facility. The aim of the subsidy is to reduce the rate of interest by 5 percent (i.e., to about 2¾ percent) for this group of countries. In order to finance the interest subsidy, contributions of approximately $85 million a year for five years are needed from the industrial and the oil-producing countries.

We welcome the extension of the IMF oil facility, particularly the establishment of the interest-subsidy arrangement for the least creditworthy developing countries. We call upon our governments as well as those of the OPEC countries to provide promptly the modest sums required to enable the interest-subsidy arrangement to function at full scale. We also urge sympathetic consideration of the extension of the facility on a scale appropriate to needs as they arise. If the interest-subsidy arrangement is continued beyond 1975, consideration should be given to financing part of it through the sale by IMF in the market of a minor portion of its gold holdings (valued officially at $6.5 billion, or $26 billion at the current market price). To conform with the Articles of Agreement, the sale would technically have to be conducted by one of the fund's members.

For financing industrial-country deficits on current account, agreement has been reached on a $25 billion mutual aid fund, or "'safety net," to be set up within the OECD framework and to be used as a last resort. The financially stronger members would provide the weaker members with credit or credit guarantees in accordance with predetermined quotas defining both lending obligations and borrowing rights. The operation will be a form of recycling to the extent that the lending countries are those that have received the most deposits and investments from the oil producers and the borrowers are those that have received the least. Like the IMF facility, the OECD arrangement will take account of the overall financial needs of members and will be conditional upon the avoidance of recourse to restrictive trade measures. However, the OECD arrangement will include more stringent conditions relating to energy-conservation and -development policies. Unlike the IMF facility, which receives funds from the oil-exporting nations and, in turn, provides these nations with an internationally guaranteed asset, the OECD arrangement does not involve any direct dealings with the OPEC countries. Thus, these countries will have to take their chances in continuing to lend and invest their surpluses in the financial markets of OECD nations.

The safety-net facility being established by the OECD countries has great merit as a form of financial insurance for a limited period in cases where private and other official recycling falls short of the needs of OECD countries. We particularly endorse the linking of mutual assistance to progress in meeting the shared objectives of lessening dependence on imported oil and maintaining a viable open international trading system. We recommend whatever authorizing action is required to put a facility such as the safety net into effect promptly.

Thus far, however, no adequate arrangement has been institutionalized in which OPEC countries would assume a major share of the credit risk of lending to countries, developing and developed alike, that are hard pressed to meet their oil-import bills. Even with the enlargement of their quotas in IMF and their World Bank subscriptions, OPEC countries will be sharing the risk of lending through these institutions only to the extent of the 10 to 15 percent represented by their shares of ownership. Individual OPEC countries have extended credits directly to a number of oil-importing countries, but these arrangements have been limited in scale, sporadic, and at terms not always suited to the financial situation of the borrower. **We recommend that the economically strong**

OECD countries try to work out with the OPEC countries a cooperative arrangement for establishing a new joint fund from which to make loans to those countries that would qualify for aid on the basis of agreed-upon economic criteria. Management of the new institution would be related to contributions and assumption of risk, but the exact proportions of OPEC and OECD contributions and the terms of the loans would be matters for negotiation. Properly set up, such an arrangement would signify the readiness of OPEC countries to assume responsibility for a fair share of the financial cost and risk involved in dealing with the consequences of their increases in oil prices.*

 CEDA (Australia) believes that the duplication of international financial institutions is unnecessary. Efforts should be made to channel the maximum amount of funds through existing multilateral agencies.

Why might OPEC countries be willing to take on the risks of lending to financially weak oil-importing countries through the intermediation of such a new international financial institution? The answer is that the alternatives open to OPEC may become less attractive as time goes on.

One alternative would be to continue to invest the bulk of their funds at short term in the banking system of the industrial countries, which would, in turn, recycle the funds in accordance with its own banking judgment. However, such investments may become much less attractive as banks reduce the interest paid on their liquid liabilities and even set limits to the amounts they are willing to accept in this form.

A second option would be longer-term investment in securities originating in OECD countries and direct investment in the industries of these countries. However, these take a considerable amount of negotiation and management, and it would be difficult to step up their volume rapidly enough to absorb the huge sums involved even with the help of specially created investment trusts.

OPEC's third option would be to reduce the output of petroleum below the currently depressed levels and in effect make a further investment in oil in the ground. However, such a strategy would make sense only if the expected future rate of price increase for oil exceeded the yield on investments abroad. At anything like the current price of oil, this would appear to be a dubious proposition. Moreover, some OPEC countries have ambitions to become local or regional powers, aspirations that entail substantial foreign exchange outlays (including expenditures on arms) which before long may begin to put pressure on their balance of payments. Another deterrent to reducing output is the fact that those OPEC countries most willing to do so (i.e., those with small populations) also have the largest reserves and therefore the greatest fear that new technologies could eventually have an unfavorable effect on the value of oil in the ground. In any case, further holding back of production could precipitate a major disturbance in the economies of OECD countries. This could jeopardize the enormous stake that OPEC will soon have accumulated in Western assets and could even lead consumer countries to desperate actions. Prudence might argue against such a policy and in favor of a compromise under which OPEC would enter into a new arrangement with the stronger industrial countries to share the ultimate risk of lending to the weaker oil-importing countries to help pay their higher petroleum-import bills.

LONG-TERM INVESTMENT OF OPEC SURPLUSES

There already is evidence of increased investment by OPEC countries in securities (including equities), in existing real assets (including real estate and businesses), and in the creation or financing of new enterprises. This trend creates a dilemma for the OECD countries. It is clearly desirable to encourage the shift of oil-country funds from destabilizing short-term commitments into longer-term, less liquid forms of investment, but a large-scale shift into equities and the direct purchase of real assets could raise the political issue of control because OPEC investments will be not only foreign investments but also foreign government investments.

Some perspective on the magnitude of this problem may be obtained by comparing the volume of OPEC surpluses with a measure of the opportunities to acquire existing long-term assets in OECD countries. The total value of stocks and bonds outstanding in the OECD countries at the end of 1972 was the equivalent of $2,900 billion, consisting of $1,700 billion in equities and $1,200 billion in bonds. The total grew at a rate of about 8.3 percent annually between 1964 and 1972. Subsequent declines in the prices of stocks and bonds traded on the securities markets have substantially slowed this growth. For the period from 1970 to 1972, the average annual value of new issues of stocks and bonds in all OECD countries was $110 billion. However, this figure fluctuates with the state of financial markets.

Even if as much as half of the current annual OPEC surpluses were invested in a cross section of outstanding OECD securities, it would amount to only about 1 percent of the total. The perceived problem arises, however, from the possible heavy concentration of OPEC investments in particular industries in particular countries through outright purchase or through the acquisition of sufficient equity to convey control. This possibility raises the kinds of fears all too familiar to American and other OECD firms that invest substantially in the economies of foreign countries. Basically, these concerns are with the influence that foreign investors may acquire over the domestic economy and with whether the foreigners will share the social responsibility that citizens have come to expect from domestic firms.

In our view, however, it would be unrealistic to expect OPEC investments in foreign enterprises to reach a scale that would seriously raise the question of influence over the national economies of OECD countries. Such investments are regarded by OPEC as potential hostages in the hands of OECD governments, a view that will restrain the extent to which this type of commitment will be pursued. **Nevertheless, the governments of the OECD countries should take whatever steps are necessary to ensure that full, systematic, and current information is available about foreign investment in their respective countries, including advance consultation in the case of major new official investments; that this information is exchanged and evaluated in OECD; and that intensified efforts are made in OECD to develop guidelines for the treatment of foreign official investments in the light of the new situation, keeping in mind the ultimate objective of securing an open world market for capital.**

In order to attract OPEC investments into long-term bonds, it is sometimes suggested that OECD governments should create special issues with such features as maintenance-of-value guarantees against inflation and devaluation. **We believe there is justification for offering special issues of government securities to OPEC countries in order to provide them with an opportunity to invest very large sums without influencing the market against themselves. But the terms of such special issues should not include guarantees that are not also made available to the general investing public.**

The standard on the basis of which foreign investment guidelines have thus far been discussed in OECD is national treatment, that is, treatment of private foreign investors equal to that accorded to investors who are nationals of the host country. But national treatment would afford little protection for foreign investment in countries where the government is the principal investor and the role of the private sector is tightly circumscribed. **In the light of the large flow of investments in both directions, consideration should be given to the desirability of substituting the principle of bilateral reciprocity for that of national treatment for investments flowing to and from countries in which the government is the principal investor.** Under the reciprocity rule, the obligation of the host country would be to treat a foreign investor in a manner equal to that accorded by his home country to a foreign investor. If national treatment were more favorable, it could be applied as a matter of discretion; but it should not be a matter of right.

IMPLICATIONS FOR INTERNATIONAL MONETARY REFORM

The abrupt change in the world monetary situation induced by the oil-price increases has affected the formal process of international monetary reform. In part because of the new uncertainties, the IMF Committee of Twenty, which was formed in July 1972, was unable to agree on a long-run reform and recommended that the changes should be achieved in an evolutionary manner. This decision is a practical recognition of the unwillingness of countries under present uncertainties to take on the new commitments required by a fully reformed international monetary system. At the same time, however, the massive deficits being incurred by the oil-consuming countries have convinced many governments that some form of exchange rate flexibility will remain a feature of the international monetary system indefinitely.

The present world payments imbalance has also underlined the importance of a cooperative approach to dealing with the problem of adjusting and financing the current account of oil-importing countries. **It is particularly important under present circumstances to press ahead with the effort to develop and agree upon more effective guidelines for managing floating currencies that would encourage consistent policies among countries and safeguard against exchange-market intervention designed to achieve unjustified competitive advantage.***

See memorandum by *FRAZAR B. WILDE, page 93.

Chapter 4

Consequences for the Developing Countries

THE PROSPECTS OF THE DEVELOPING COUNTRIES have changed drastically from those anticipated prior to the oil-price increases late in 1973. In considering their altered situation, however, two points need to be borne in mind: first, the highly differentiated character of the developing world and, second, the fact that the oil-price increases are only one element (although a major one) in a more complex set of interrelated circumstances affecting the economies of the developing world.

At least three groups of countries must be distinguished within the Third World: oil-exporting countries, developing countries with annual per capita incomes above $200, and developing countries with per capita incomes below $200. The 280 million people in the OPEC countries are clearly in a greatly improved position to benefit from the vastly increased earnings from their oil exports. Since 1974, this group of countries has accounted for more than half the total value of the developing world's exports. However, this chapter is primarily concerned with the last two groups. They are differentiated by income levels and by their access to external capital and the extent to which the increases in their oil-import bills have been offset by favorable developments in prices and markets for their principal exports. Many countries in the second group have partially financed the heavy 1974 oil deficits and avoided severe deterioration of growth rates because their foreign exchange reserves have benefited from buoyant export prices (e.g., Thailand and the Philippines) or because of a substantial potential for the export of industrial goods (e.g., Brazil and Korea). The countries in the third group are the least able to cope with the new situation. They include the nations of South Asia (Bangladesh, India, Pakistan, and Sri Lanka) and a number of countries in eastern and central Africa (Ethiopia, Kenya, Mali, Sudan, Tanzania, and Uganda) and have a total population of about 800 million people.

Closely related to the oil-price increases have been other elements in the international economic situation that must be considered in assessing the outlook for developing countries: the steep increases in 1973 and 1974 in the price of food and strategic development materials with a high energy content, especially nitrogenous fertilizers, the high prices in 1973 and 1974 of many primary commodities that helped to offset the oil-price increases for some exporting developing countries but that exacerbated the foreign exchange stringency for others; the continued worldwide inflation that increases the costs less developed countries must pay for imports of manufactured goods and that creates uncertainty for development planning and investment decisions; and the slowdown in the rate of growth of the industrial countries (aggravated by the adjustment to higher oil prices) that are the principal markets for the exports of developing countries. In addition, rapid population growth continues to drain the resources of the less developed countries and to act as a drag on their development.

INCREASED COST OF OIL AND RELATED IMPORTS

For most poor countries, foreign exchange is a major constraint on development. Yet, the increase in oil prices cost developing countries that are not members of OPEC approximately $10 billion in 1974, or about 11 percent of their overall imports in that year. This is almost equal to the total official development assistance in 1974 of all sixteen member countries of OECD participating in DAC. Although an examination of all payments items is required in order to assess the burden that fuel imports impose on a country's balance of payments, the absorption of a sharply increased share of foreign exchange by oil imports is bound to affect development prospects adversely.

As we have noted, the most severely affected countries are in South Asia and Africa. Higher oil prices added $800 million to India's import bill in 1974, an amount equal to approximately two-thirds of its entire foreign exchange reserves at the end of 1973, more than 25 percent of its total exports, and considerably more than official capital inflows net of debt service. Sri Lanka paid $100 million more for petroleum imports in 1974 than in 1973; at the same time, it was confronted with deteriorating terms of trade because the price of its major export, tea, had been stagnating. The new oil prices added $70 million to the import costs of Bangladesh at a time when floods devastated the countryside and augmented the country's import bill for minimum food needs. For the most severely affected countries of Africa, the quadrupled oil prices drove the cost of essential fuel imports from 10 percent of export earnings to 30 or 40 percent at the same time that the most devastating drought in history drastically increased their requirements for imported food to stave off mass starvation.

The direct effects of the oil-price increases were aggravated, particularly for the poorer developing countries, by the shortages and high prices of fertilizers and food. The price of urea fertilizer rose almost as rapidly as that of crude oil; even at $250 a ton, many developing countries were unable to obtain as much in 1974 as in the previous crop year, thus retarding the progress of the so-called green revolution. The shortages were due to a combination of the increased need for fertilizer for the miracle grains, a lag in the construction of new production facilities, and cutbacks in fertilizer output (especially in Japan) as a result of the oil shortage. The high price of food grains also meant heavy increases in foreign exchange expenditures for food imports. In total, the developing countries had to pay an additional $5 billion for food and fertilizer imports in crop year 1973–74. The populous countries of the Indian subcontinent, which have the least flexibility in meeting the additional costs of oil imports, are also those which rely heavily on fertilizer imports and whose food production is highly sensitive to inadequate soil nutrients.

The prospects for relieving the balance-of-payments pressures of developing countries through internal adjustments to higher energy costs are not promising in the medium term. Some reduction in consumption may be possible through greater efficiency and conservation in energy use, but the scope for such saving is small. The countries with per capita incomes below $200 consume only about 1 percent as much energy per capita as the United States; thus, it is doubtful that a significant reduction can be accomplished without leading to lower agricultural and industrial production and a decline in the standard of living.

The prospects are better for reducing imports of petroleum by substituting domestic sources of energy. A promising Indian example is the Gobar gas units based on "agri-waste." They produce methane gas for cooking, lighting, and transportation at the same time that nitrogen is returned to the soil. In India, Pakistan, and other developing countries, it should also be possible to replace petroleum-based power plants with hydropower or with coal, lignite, or nuclear fuel plants. But it will take at least a half-dozen years before such prospects can become operational. And the large additional investments they require will draw resources away from other projects, thereby reducing the countries' development programs.

OUTLOOK FOR EXPORT EARNINGS

The capacity of those developing countries that are not oil producers to bear the higher cost of imports of oil and other essential products depends first of all on the outlook for their export earnings. Although exports of manufactured goods have grown rapidly since 1960, primary products still constitute 60 percent of their exports. Therefore, the prospects of primary-product markets for the rest of this decade will heavily condition the ability of developing countries to cope with the new world energy situation.

The unfavorable trend in the developing countries' terms of trade that had existed since the end of the Korean War was reversed by the commodity boom which began in the latter part of 1972. The rise in prices reflected the effects of both an unusually rapid acceleration of overall demand and shortages of particular commodities as a result of climatic and other conditions. Now that the boom has ended, the main question is whether commodity markets are likely to return to their former adverse trends over the medium and longer term or whether 1973 and 1974 mark the beginning of a period of growing shortages and high prices. Ideally, the answer to this question should be based on separate examinations of the situation in each commodity market, a task clearly beyond the scope of this statement. Nevertheless, some general observations can be offered.*

From the standpoint of demand, the principal determinant of the market outlook for exports of primary commodities is the anticipated GNP growth of the OECD countries. The sharp reduction in growth in 1974 contributed to a softening of some commodity prices, and no recovery of GNP growth is forecast by the OECD Secretariat for 1975. Given present uncertainties and the greater complexity of financial management as a result of the oil situation, it is questionable whether total OECD growth can be sustained at 5 percent (the average rate in real terms that prevailed during the period from 1960 to 1973) during the period from 1976 to 1980. World demand conditions, therefore, are unlikely to provide an upward thrust to the commodity markets of developing countries and may well turn out to have a depressing effect.

From the standpoint of long-run supply, the main limits to world output of primary materials are the availability of arable land and of specific mineral resources. Some studies suggest that there are only a

See memorandum by *R. HEATH LARRY, page 96.

small number of commodities for which conditions of world supply relative to demand are likely to lead to an increase in relative prices (i.e., prices in relation to a general index of international prices) over those of 1960. Implicit in this assessment, however, is the assumption that there are only limited possibilities for raising prices through producer alliances such as OPEC.

Therefore, when the principal factors affecting the prospective demand and supply situation for primary materials other than petroleum are taken into account, it appears unlikely that there will be an increase in the export earnings of developing countries sufficient to offset the increased cost of petroleum and, for some countries, food. Moreover, the effects of sluggish export markets on the developing countries' capacity to import are likely to be exacerbated by the persistent inflation in the OECD countries reflected in the rapidly rising prices of the manufactured and capital goods that developing countries must import.

The combined prospects of rising prices for imports of manufactured products and weakened export markets for their primary products mean the likelihood of a resumption of the adverse long-term movement in the developing countries' terms of trade. At the same time, the rapid inflation is having various side effects on them. Some are unfavorable, such as the reduction in the real value of the already inadequate amounts of aid flowing to them. Others are favorable, such as the easing of the real burden of the developing countries' debt-servicing and repayment obligations.

AID REQUIREMENTS

Recently, the World Bank attempted to estimate the increased capital requirements of the developing countries in the face of the new situation in the world economy. It concluded that even the most optimistic projections of capital flows made before the oil-price increases would now be utterly inadequate to sustain acceptable rates of growth. Minimum acceptable growth is defined by the bank as a continuing growth in per capita GNP of 4 percent for developing countries with per capita incomes over $200 and 2 percent for those with per capita incomes under $200. For those developing countries (excluding mainland China) with per capita incomes below $200 and a total population of 800 million, the previously projected flows of assistance would not be sufficient to ward off the appalling prospect of a decline in per capita incomes.

When the complex adjustment of the world economy to inflation and higher energy costs is taken into account, the need for development assistance increases substantially. According to the World Bank, aid requirements on concessionary terms to achieve minimum acceptable growth rates will rise from $12 billion in 1973 to $30 billion in 1980. In addition, borrowing by developing countries on market terms will need to rise from approximately $9 billion in 1973 to $24 billion in 1980. Of these required increases in net capital flows, a substantial portion will simply offset the higher prices of goods and services imported by the developing countries.

FINANCE AT MARKET TERMS

There is at least a reasonable chance that many middle- and higher-income developing countries can meet their needs for funds at market terms by borrowing in the Eurocurrency market, by resort to the IMF oil facility, and by borrowing from the hard-loan windows of international development finance institutions, especially the World Bank.

Eurocurrency credits received by developing countries have been substantial. They amounted to $6 billion in the first half of 1974 but tapered off to $3.5 billion in the second half and continued at that rate in the first quarter of 1975. The borrowing of very large amounts by industrialized countries does not appear to have impaired the access of the more creditworthy developing countries to this market. Although Eurocurrency borrowing by developing countries continues to be dominated in terms of volume by a small number of countries with relatively high incomes, twenty-eight developing countries resorted to this source of funds in 1974. Eurocurrency credits customarily carry a floating interest rate, and most have been for terms of seven to ten years. If the central banks of developed countries stand behind the Eurocurrency banks as lenders of last resort, this market should be in a position to continue to play a role (although a more limited one) in recycling oil surpluses to the more creditworthy developing countries.

We have already referred to the IMF oil facility as an intermediary in recycling funds to oil-importing countries. Although Italy was the largest single borrower from the facility in 1974, more than $1.2 billion was loaned to developing countries. With the expansion of the oil facility and the enlargement of normal drawing facilities as a result of increased quotas, IMF will be a prime source of medium-term credits to enable developing countries to meet their current account deficits over the critical period to 1980.

The World Bank should become an important intermediary in re-cycling oil money at longer term, especially to developing countries that do not have the standing to borrow directly in private financial markets but that are nevertheless in a position to assume additional debt-service obligations according to the conditions established for the bank's hard-loan window. In order to finance these operations, the bank should be in a position to borrow large sums from the oil-exporting countries. In fact, the bank is already an established borrower from a number of OPEC countries; its borrowing history dates back to 1968 in the case of Saudi Arabia. In addition, it has sold substantial issues of bonds in Kuwait, Libya, Oman, Abu Dhabi, and Venezuela. Iran, which has itself been a borrower from the bank, has indicated a willingness to purchase bank bonds substantially in excess of any bank commitments of funds to Iran.

In addition to borrowing directly from the oil-exporting countries, the World Bank will need to mobilize surplus oil revenues indirectly by selling bonds in the capital markets of OECD countries. The distribution of bank borrowings in these countries will, of course, be conditional upon the pattern of flows of surplus oil revenues and the consequent balance-of-payments positions of individual OECD countries. However, the bank must receive permission from any member country in whose currency it wishes to borrow. **We recommend that the World Bank also be enabled to mobilize oil revenues indirectly by being granted ready access to OECD capital markets.**

CONCESSIONARY AID*

Much more difficult than meeting the requirements of the developing countries for finance on market terms is the problem of providing for the estimated increase in their concessionary aid requirements from $12 billion in 1973 to $30 billion in 1980. It is out of this soft money that the needs of the poorest and least creditworthy developing countries must be met. Given the low interest rates on concessionary loans, long maturities, and the probable inflationary erosion of the principal, a large portion of such lending should be viewed effectively as grants.

Some OPEC countries have made a substantial start in committing funds to this group of developing countries, mostly through bilateral arrangements. However, the terms and conditions of these commitments are not always made generally known, nor is it always clear whether they are intended to be one-time or continuing operations. In addition to grants

See memorandum by *G. BARRON MALLORY, page 93.

and low-interest loans, assistance from OPEC members could, to a greater extent than heretofore, take the form of lower prices for oil sold to the poorest developing countries or of repayment in local currency.

We have already noted our approval of the new interest-subsidy arrangement of the IMF oil facility, which will make it possible for the fund to extend medium-term credit on concessionary terms to the poorest developing countries. **The interest-subsidy technique will also be used to enable the World Bank to establish a "third window" for making long-term loans at rates in between those charged for the bank's hard loans and those charged for the very soft loans of its International Development Association (IDA). We recommend that our governments contribute the sums necessary to enable such a "third window" to operate on a modest initial scale as a means of increasing the World Bank's flexibility in assisting developing countries that require concessionary finance.**

However, we see IDA as playing the central role in helping the poorest and least creditworthy developing countries. The terms of IDA credits amount to grants for 75 percent of their face value even without taking into account the inflationary erosion of the principal. **We urge contributions to the International Development Association by the member governments of both OPEC and OECD in amounts sufficient to enable the poorest countries to sustain acceptable rates of growth.**

Whatever form concessionary lending takes, a key question is how the total amount of necessary concessionary lending should be shared by OPEC and OECD countries. We therefore propose what might be a reasonable basis for dealing with the foreign exchange gap of developing countries that require concessionary assistance. Those OPEC countries with higher per capita incomes might contribute concessionary aid in amounts related to the additional price of petroleum paid by other developing countries; OECD countries might be asked to increase their flows of grants and soft loans in amounts related to the increased costs of imports of other goods and services paid by the developing countries.

It is sometimes argued that because OECD countries have higher per capita incomes than OPEC countries, they should assist the developing countries in paying the increased price of oil. However, it is important to differentiate among OPEC countries. Most of the surplus oil revenues are being accumulated by a group of sparsely populated countries with high per capita incomes: Saudi Arabia, Kuwait, Libya, Qatar, and the United Arab Emirates. Their per capita income of $4,200 in 1974 is at the same level as that of Western Europe and exceeds that of Japan. A second group of OPEC countries (Algeria, Iraq, Iran, and Venezuela) has achieved a per capita income of $1,200, a level three times higher than the average for other developing countries. They are in the same range as Ireland, Spain, and Yugoslavia, countries that have elected to contribute to IDA. The remaining OPEC members (Indonesia and Nigeria) are at half the average income level of other developing countries and should not be expected to contribute. In short, OPEC's contributions to concessionary assistance should come mainly from the first group of countries, with only relatively small contributions from the second group.

Conversely, it may be argued that OPEC should finance a share of the increase in import requirements attributable to inflation because the oil-price increase has contributed to the inflationary spiral. As we have noted, however, this contribution has been less than one-half of the total. Most of the inflationary pressure comes from within the OECD area itself. It seems unreasonable, therefore, to ask OPEC countries to cover any more of the inflationary increase in aid requirements than they would already be doing with respect to oil if this proposal is accepted.

A compromise along the lines we have suggested could be constructed on the assumption that the flow of concessionary aid from OECD countries to developing countries will keep step with inflation. Using the World Bank's projected price deflator for imports of developmental goods, OECD assistance would rise from approximately $12 billion in 1973 to $22 billion by 1980. If the remainder of the bank's projected requirements for concessionary aid ($30 billion in 1980) were made up by OPEC countries, their contribution would amount to $8 billion. This is somewhat less than the increase in the developing countries' 1974 oil-import bill as compared with their 1973 bill.

Chapter 5

International Trade Policy

AMONG THE MORE URGENT international economic questions precipitated by the energy crisis are five issues of trade policy: the use of trade measures in cases of balance-of-payments disequilibrium, new international rules on export controls, the question of politically motivated restrictions on exports, the future role of producer cartels and intergovernmental commodity agreements, and the implications of the trend toward more processing of raw materials in producing countries.

TRADE MEASURES
FOR BALANCE-OF-PAYMENTS ADJUSTMENT

This issue has come to the fore as a result of the unprecedented change in the structure of world payments following the increase in oil prices. Because of the deterioration of the current accounts of most OECD countries, the temptation will be strong to resort to unilateral trade measures to improve national competitive positions. A case in point is the action taken by Italy in May 1974 to require advance import deposits as a means of coping with its deteriorating payments position. Partly in reaction to the Italian measure, members of OECD subsequently adopted a declaration that they would, for one year, avoid trying to deal with the consequences of the oil situation through unilateral trade measures. The declaration was renewed in May 1975. In addition, the six major OECD countries (France, West Germany, Italy, Japan, the United Kingdom, and the United States) have agreed to end export credits extending beyond three years to each other and to the wealthy oil-producing states. The agreement also establishes a 7.5 percent floor to interest rates on export credits to other countries.

Nevertheless, the role that trade measures such as quantitative restrictions, import surcharges and deposits, and export subsidies should play in balance-of-payments adjustment and the type of international constraints that should be placed on their use remain open to question. Such measures lead to distortions on both the domestic and the international levels. The greatest distortions are caused by quantitative restrictions because they involve the most complete break with the market mechanism. For the individual countries concerned, trade measures are only expedients; they do not create a durable equilibrium. From the standpoint of the international community, the objection to trade measures is that they shift the burden of adjusting a country's external deficit directly onto the economies of its trading partners. Moreover, the effects of such measures can be sudden and severe and can lead other countries to retaliate, triggering a cycle of restrictions and counterrestrictions.

Although these disadvantages are generally recognized, trade measures may nevertheless have a certain appeal over other actions. When the deficit is very large, countries may be loath to pursue corrective policies entirely by internal measures because the necessary degree of deflation may be judged excessive in social and political as well as in economic terms. Measures directly affecting the trade balance may then reduce the extent of deflation that is required.*

Under the existing system of flexible exchange rates, the case for trade measures in adjusting balance-of-payments deficits is obviously diminished; changes in rates can more readily be allowed to carry the burden of adjustment. But countries may still prefer trade measures because of the time required for an exchange rate change to affect the flow of trade and the further concern that under certain circumstances currency depreciation may be more inflationary.

It would be unrealistic therefore to expect countries to agree to an absolute prohibition of the use of trade measures for balance-of-payments purposes. Instead, effort should be concentrated on ways of limiting recourse to trade measures and of ensuring that the distortion of trade and the damage to a country's trading partners are minimized when such measures are adopted.

The present multilateral system for dealing with trade measures to protect the balance of payments has been outdated for a long time. Although GATT permits the use of quantitative trade restrictions to safeguard the position of a deficit country, rarely has any major trading country in fact resorted to them since the beginning of the general movement to restore currency convertibility in the late 1950s. On the other

See memorandum by *R. HEATH LARRY, page 96.

hand, import surcharges and export subsidies, which violate GATT's tariff commitments and subsidy provisions, respectively, have been applied on a number of occasions.

A further anomaly resides in the procedural and institutional arrangements for giving international sanction to trade measures to protect the balance of payments. Under GATT, a country is free to apply quantitative trade restrictions without prior approval and subject only to a requirement for ex post facto consultation. Under the IMF Articles of Agreement, however, a member may not impose exchange restrictions on current transactions (including payments for imports) without prior approval of the fund's executive board. Nevertheless, a quantitative exchange restriction applied to imports of goods can be the same in all practical respects as a quantitative trade restriction.

The General Agreement on Tariffs and Trade (GATT) and the IMF Articles of Agreement should be amended to permit countries in balance-of-payments difficulties to use appropriate trade measures in addition to quotas, but any such measure should be subject to more stringent IMF surveillance of its justification on balance-of-payments grounds. At the same time, GATT would retain jurisdiction over the acceptability of the restriction in terms of commercial policy (e.g., compliance with the rule on nondiscrimination, avoidance of unnecessary damage to the trading partners, and allowing the importation of commercial samples).* *

 KEIZAI DOYUKAI (Japan) dissents from this recommendation. Such amendments to GATT articles as are suggested here will require revisions not only of Article XII dealing with quantitative import restrictions but also of many other articles. This will inevitably present some complex problems that will have far-reaching impacts on the international trade system. Furthermore, Keizai Doyukai believes that IMF articles should not be revised before we have a more stable climate in the world economy.

NEW INTERNATIONAL RULES ON EXPORT CONTROLS

The oil embargo in the winter of 1973–1974 dramatized a major gap in the system of multilateral rules governing international trade policy.

See memorandum by *HERMAN L. WEISS, page 94.

Until recently, trade policy concentrated on improving access to markets through the reduction or elimination of import restrictions, but it paid little attention to the question of ensuring access to supplies by limiting the possibility of imposing export restraints. Among the main reasons for export restrictions have been short supplies, political or national security considerations, and the desire to influence world prices.

Although oil was the main catalyst in bringing this issue to the fore-front of policy concerns, the problem began to emerge earlier as shortages and skyrocketing prices appeared in a whole series of basic commodities. In response to rapidly rising meat prices in the United States, the government instituted in June 1973 a temporary embargo on soybean exports, replacing it shortly thereafter with a system of export licensing designed to reduce U.S. sales abroad. At about the same time, other scarce commodities, including iron and steel scrap, chemical fertilizers, and timber, also became subject to export restraints in a number of supplying countries.

There is wide support for more effective GATT rules governing export restrictions in situations of short supply. Contrary to the popular conception, trade in primary products does not fall into a neat developed-versus-developing-country pattern. Although developing countries are the major exporters of most minerals and agricultural raw materials, they are, on balance, importers rather than exporters of basic food grains. In fact, for many years, the prospects are that their need for access to sources from which to import grains will increase rather than diminish. Hence, there is a worldwide common interest in subjecting restrictions on access to supplies to more effective international constraints than those now provided under GATT. **In the new round of trade negotiations, every effort should be made to establish clearly defined provisions on export restrictions. The main objectives should be to ensure international consultation before export restrictions are used to meet shortage situations, to define permissible measures restricting exports, to give effect to the principle of equitable sharing, and to encourage the development of positive and constructive export programs rather than restrictive measures to cope with shortages over the longer term.**

POLITICALLY MOTIVATED EXPORT RESTRICTIONS

The Arab oil embargo in late 1973 and early 1974 was an example of a politically motivated export restriction. Included in the same category, however, are the OECD strategic-trade controls and the U.S. embargo on exports to Cuba.

No effective international constraints on the use of trade restrictions for political security exist today. Although GATT outlaws export restrictions, the rule is subject to a variety of exceptions; the most sweeping of these is the national security article. This article permits a country to take any action it considers necessary to protect its "essential security interests" not only during wartime but also during any other unilaterally determined "emergency in international relations."

Except for Kuwait, the main petroleum-exporting countries that participated in the recent restrictions on oil exports for political purposes are not now parties to GATT. However, as these countries begin to industrialize, membership in GATT should become more attractive to them.

Whether it would be possible to negotiate within GATT or another forum a tighter national security provision that would effectively limit embargoes and other forms of politically motivated restrictions on access to supplies is open to serious question, given the sensitivity of countries to any constraints on their freedom of action in matters affecting national security.

PRODUCER CARTELS AND COMMODITY AGREEMENTS

Export arrangements may be designed to influence world market prices through either a producer cartel (such as OPEC) or an international commodity agreement (such as the tin agreement) in which both producers and consumers participate. Arrangements of this sort have had a long and checkered history since the early 1900s. But it was not until the period immediately following World War II that a concerted worldwide attempt was made to establish a comprehensive set of principles relating to both international cartels and commodity agreements. This was done in the Havana Charter for the International Trade Organization (ITO), drawn up in 1948 but never officially put into effect.

All that remains of the ITO effort to deal comprehensively with international cartels and commodity agreements is an oblique reference in GATT Article XX-h to the admissibility of any trade measures, including export restrictions, that are adopted to carry out intergovernmental commodity agreements conforming to the general principles of the chapter on commodity agreements included in the draft charter of ITO. Given the wide divergence of views on this emotionally charged subject, it is highly doubtful that any new and more explicit attempt to legislate comprehensive international rules on cartels or commodity agreements would meet with success today.

As it stands, however, Article XX-h of GATT does in effect require that intergovernmental commodity agreements involving restrictions on trade conform to the criterion of equitable representation of consuming and producing countries alike in the negotiation and administration of the agreement. Agreements among producing countries only that involve trade restrictions are therefore in violation of GATT. **We believe that multilateral arrangements on certain internationally traded commodities consistent with the GATT criterion of equitable representation may serve a useful purpose in moderating sharp fluctuations in the prices of primary products and in preventing arbitrary interruptions of supply. A more positive attitude toward such arrangements on the part of the OECD governments might help to deter the present tendency toward the formation of producer cartels.***

However, the main safeguard against the concerted exercise of monopoly power in primary materials is the inherent difficulty of organizing and sustaining restrictive producer arrangements. One of the main requirements for a successful producer cartel is inelastic demand for the relevant commodity with respect to price, preferably in both the long and the short runs. This implies that the commodity is an essential good for which there is no readily available substitute (including alternative sources of supply) at competitive prices. An additional practical requirement is that relatively few countries should control a large proportion of the supply entering the world market. Otherwise, the problem of restricting total output becomes extremely difficult because smaller producers are often tempted to exceed their quotas at the high prices. These conditions severely limit the prospects of other producer alliances modeled on OPEC. A number of previous attempts at exporter cartels in such varied commodities as coffee, cocoa, copper, and bananas have failed. Whether renewed efforts for products such as copper, bauxite, iron ore, and some agricultural products will prove more successful remains to be seen, but it seems inherently improbable.

Moreover, OPEC's success in raising prices and maintaining them at a high level may be attributed to a number of special circumstances in addition to low price elasticity of demand and high concentration of export supply. First, U.S. production began to decline in 1970; at about the same time, actions to protect the environment prompted increased

See memorandum by *HERMAN L. WEISS, page 94.

oil consumption and placed additional constraints on domestic production. As a result, world demand for internationally traded oil soared. Second, governments of key exporting countries (especially Saudi Arabia, Libya, and Kuwait) have been financially strong enough to accept the lower levels of petroleum exports necessary to maintain a given high price even in the absence of comparable restraints on the part of other oil exporters. Third, the taxes and royalties levied on the international oil companies by OPEC established an effective floor to prices. Fourth, low labor intensity makes it possible for the exporting countries to vary production levels without causing domestic social and political stress. Fifth, the Arab-Israeli conflict provided an important shared political objective for a major segment of the oil-exporting nations that overcame other political and psychological reservations.

Despite these favorable circumstances, strains within OPEC will appear to the degree that energy conservation and new sources of supply affect the market for OPEC oil. The test will come if agreement on market shares should become necessary in order to support the world price. No serious attempt at such an agreement has yet been made. The smaller exporters who depend heavily on oil revenues for current expenditures might oppose more than nominal constraints on output. Moreover, OPEC's cohesiveness will be affected by the diversity of economic interests as well as the sharp political conflicts and rivalries among its members. Exporting countries with large reserves (such as Saudi Arabia and the United Arab Emirates) tend to think in longer-term perspectives than countries with more limited reserves (such as Algeria, Venezuela, Nigeria, and even Iran). The former are naturally less inclined to support a price that would reduce oil consumption and encourage alternative sources of energy. Differences on price policy such as that between Saudi Arabia and Iran have already surfaced at recent OPEC meetings and in public statements by officials of the two governments.

An alternative approach to regulating the world oil market would be an international commodity agreement involving the principal exporters and importers. The two groups of countries would have to agree on a price range, and both would have to undertake commitments to support it, the exporters by contracting to produce enough to prevent the price from exceeding the ceiling and the importers by helping to enforce assigned export quotas to prevent prices from falling below the floor. In principle, both groups could benefit substantially. Exporters would presumably have to accept some price reduction in the short term in return for long-term price floors and a larger export market. Importers would be reinforcing the ability of the exporters to maintain prices by allocating market shares in return for short-term price reductions and long-term price ceilings. If importers were sufficiently confident about the reliability of the arrangement, they could perhaps also pare their commitments somewhat to invest in alternative higher-cost sources of energy. But such a decision would involve a difficult trade-off between long-term security of supply and some economic gain.

An international commodity agreement on oil would involve formidable negotiating problems, both between exporters and importers and among the members of each group, in reaching decisions on a price range, export quotas, benefits for new exporters, and enforcement mechanisms. Beyond the technical difficulties lie mutual suspicions and different assessments of bargaining leverage.

When the atmosphere improves, however, the advantages of a cooperative multilateral approach may prove sufficiently appealing to make it a feasible way of ordering world trade in petroleum. It may then be possible to negotiate a mutually beneficial commodity agreement on oil that will include provisions on price, supply, or other factors. Such an arrangement would need to be flexible enough to allow prices to be adjusted as market conditions change. It should be recognized, however, that difficult theoretical and practical problems are involved in determining the long-run supply price for exhaustible resources. **We do not regard indexing—that is, a system of linking the price of oil to the price of other goods—as an appropriate principle for setting the price of oil or other commodities because it would stimulate inflation and rigidify prices on a basis that is unrelated to market conditions, including long-term trends in technology.** *

 IDEP (France) believes that the rejection of indexing should be seen against a background in which each country (producer or consumer) is struggling to control inflation and all feel themselves to be allied in this effort and are taking similar actions, although with due allowance for their respective situations.

PROCESSING OIL AND OTHER RAW MATERIALS
IN PRODUCING COUNTRIES

Developing countries that export raw materials have increasingly sought to process their resources locally for supply to the world market. In the case of oil, some producing countries have ambitious plans to develop not only substantial local refining capacity but also national petrochemical industries based on domestically produced oil and gas.

Local processing is viewed by most producing countries as a natural path to development. In addition to augmenting foreign exchange earnings, it increases employment, provides opportunities to upgrade the skills of the work force, and stimulates ancillary industrial activities. In the case of petroleum, local refining facilities also provide a domestic outlet for investing surplus oil revenues. Although petroleum refining and the processing of mineral ores are highly capital intensive and therefore likely to lead to only modest direct increases in employment, they appear to go some way toward fulfilling national aspirations. Particularly in industries that are highly concentrated internationally, local processing is regarded as an important means of achieving a measure of economic independence from traditional markets.

From the point of view of consuming countries, two issues are involved: one relating to security, the other to commercial policy. The security problem results from the increased vulnerability of consuming countries to an interruption of supplies when they depend not only on foreign sources of raw materials but also on foreign processing-plant capacity. Alternative sources of raw materials may be readily available, but plant capacity may take several years to build. Clearly, the trend toward local processing has implications for the consuming countries in terms of the need to stockpile both processed and raw materials and to maintain reserve plant capacity.

The commercial policy issue raised by the local processing of raw materials concerns the terms of entry for processed products on the markets of consuming countries. At present, the tariff structure in most OECD countries discriminates against products at early stages of processing. Typically, raw materials enter duty-free, but processed products bear duties that escalate with the stage of processing. Even when the nominal tariff on the processed product is low, the effective protection on the value added in processing may be very high. Hypothetically, for example, if crude oil, constituting 80 percent of the value of oil products, enters a country duty-free but oil products are subject to a tariff of 10 percent, then the effective protection on the refining of the crude oil (i.e., on the 20 percent value added to the crude) is, not 10 percent, but 50 percent. This is the true measure of the extent to which a domestic refiner could exceed the world market costs of refining crude oil into products.

As new capacity for processing raw materials is needed, local processing in developing countries should be encouraged as a legitimate part of a strategy of development. This encouragement should be subject to the economic feasibility of specific projects and consistent with the need to ensure stable supplies of processed products. We recommend that in the forthcoming trade negotiations a special effort be made to reduce the degree of tariff discrimination against imports of processed products. In the case of strategic materials, such liberalization should be subject to adequate safeguards in forms such as stockpiles of processed products in the importing countries and adequate reserve capacity for processing.

Chapter 6

International Cooperation in Energy Demand and Supply

THE PRECEDING CHAPTERS are addressed primarily to ways in which the oil-consuming countries can cope over the short and medium term with the tremendous upheaval in the international economic system brought on by the increases in the price of oil since the latter part of 1973. Regardless of the financial schemes that are devised, however, the adjustment to the new situation in the energy market over the period until 1980 will unavoidably entail huge transfers of income and wealth to the OPEC countries, the piling up of tremendous debts by many oil-consuming countries, and the threatening shadow of financial collapse for the weaker importing countries.

Unless strong measures are quickly taken to alter the basic demand and supply relationships in the international oil market, these conditions will persist beyond 1980 because the oil-importing countries will remain vulnerable to unrestrained increases in the price of oil and interruptions in its supply. Prompt and coordinated steps among the industrial countries are therefore essential to consolidate contingency plans for emergency conditions, to conserve the use of energy, and to develop alternative domestic and imported supplies of energy.

Today, only two OECD countries are self-sufficient in energy supplies: Norway and Canada. The United Kingdom may become self-sufficient by about 1980 when its North Sea oil comes on-stream; and if Project Independence is followed vigorously, the dependence of the United States on energy imports may be reduced to perhaps 10 percent by 1985. But as Figure 4 demonstrates, other industrial countries are heavily dependent on imported energy; in fact, most industrial countries cannot hope to achieve a degree of energy self-sufficiency equal to that now being sought by the United States. The goal for every country should thus be energy *security*, a situation in which dependence on uncertain

FIGURE 4: DEPENDENCE ON IMPORTED ENERGY, BY SELECTED COUNTRIES, 1973

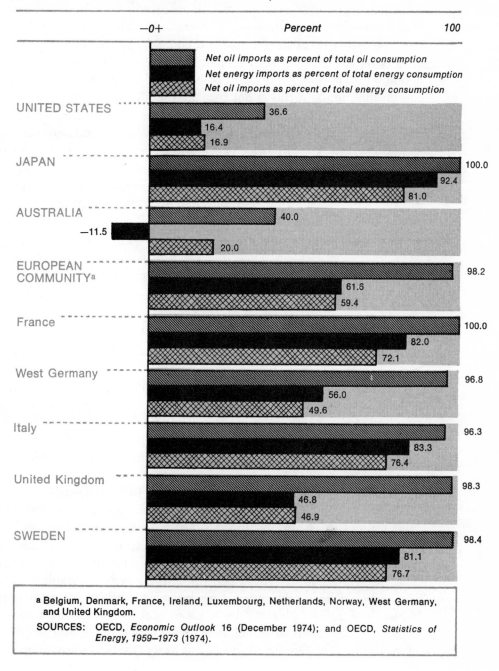

a Belgium, Denmark, France, Ireland, Luxembourg, Netherlands, Norway, West Germany, and United Kingdom.

SOURCES: OECD, *Economic Outlook* 16 (December 1974); and OECD, *Statistics of Energy, 1959–1973* (1974).

foreign sources is reduced to the extent that supply interruptions can be met without unacceptable economic, social, or political costs.

Although energy security will be achieved essentially by the actions of individual nations, there are important reasons why national policies should be adopted in an international context and should take advantage of the scope for international cooperation. Individual countries have little option but to accept the high oil prices and the uncertainty of the global energy situation, but this is not true for the oil-consuming countries as a whole. Cooperative measures to share oil in emergencies, to conserve energy, and to develop new sources can affect the world energy situation, including OPEC's future price expectations and possibly its present price policies. Stimulated by recent events, all countries are formulating comprehensive national energy plans. Both their cost and the time needed to put them into effect may be reduced if they are integrated with international actions right from the start.

BILATERAL DEALS

In the wake of the OPEC price increases and supply cutbacks of late 1973, many oil-importing countries rushed into special bilateral deals with oil-exporting countries in an effort to assure themselves of adequate and reasonably secure energy supplies. The arrangements (a number of which have lapsed) provided for the exchange of industrial products, technical assistance, and sometimes arms in return for long-term commitments to supply specified quantities of oil. Such deals, particularly those initiated by the countries most heavily dependent on imported energy, were an understandable reaction to the trauma of the first phase of the oil crisis.

However, as a general long-run strategy for oil-importing countries, the bilateral approach carries certain dangers. As countries seek to preempt sources of oil supply through discriminatory arrangements and to tie up oil-country markets through privileged access, they run the risk of bidding up prices and stabilizing them at a higher level. At the same time, each individual country could end up with no more favorable treatment than it would have received in the absence of the special arrangement. Moreover, specific long-term deals are subject to abrogation if economic or political conditions should change or if a new crisis should erupt in the oil-exporting area. Finally, the costs and strains for the entire international economic community are likely to be serious because a go-it-alone strategy undermines the multilateral system of principles and institutions that has evolved over the past thirty years.

Nevertheless, given the diversity of the energy-supply situation in oil-importing industrial countries, it is inevitable that national initiatives will include various forms of bilateral arrangements with oil exporters. Under these circumstances, we see a role for OECD or some other appropriate organization in improving the bargaining position of its members in obtaining oil on more favorable terms. Pooling information on bilateral deals would reduce the chances of any importing country acting with inadequate knowledge of market conditions. Furthermore, by subjecting bilateral deals to mutual discussion and guidelines among member countries, OECD could exercise some restraint on arrangements that bid up prices unnecessarily or tie up supplies or markets excessively.

However, the basic long-run strategy for holding oil prices down and preventing interruptions of supply must lie in more fundamental efforts to moderate the rise in demand and to increase alternative supplies of energy. Such programs for energy conservation and development offer considerable scope for cooperative action. In addition, joint planning is essential to meet short-run emergency situations through measures such as stockpiling, reserve capacity, and the sharing of existing supplies.

COOPERATION IN EMERGENCIES

The disruption caused by the general and selective oil embargoes during the winter of 1973–1974 demonstrated the need for international agreement on mutual assistance during emergencies caused by supply interruptions.

Requirements for an International Agreement. An international agreement must include a clear definition of an emergency situation, stockpiling and conservation commitments, and plans to activate shut-in capacity and reallocate supplies among consuming countries. To the maximum extent, such an agreement must be both explicit and automatic if it is to protect all countries subscribing to it and to act as a deterrent to any supply cutoff by producing countries.

The extent of the required program depends on expectations regarding possible emergencies. The diverse characteristics of the members of OPEC make it unlikely that all of them would simultaneously impose even a selective embargo. Quite apart from the different political and foreign policy views of the OPEC members, the costs of any embargo would not be distributed equally among them. For example, the United States imports almost two-thirds of Venezuela's oil exports; Venezuela would therefore suffer more than the Middle Eastern countries if OPEC as a whole were to embargo the United States.

Their common antipathy toward Israel makes the Arab countries the most likely group within OPEC to impose an embargo on the industrial world. The effect that an embargo on oil exports by those countries would have would differ from industrial nation to nation. Europe and Japan would bear the brunt of any general embargo of the industrial countries. The United States is less dependent on imports but is seriously deficient in storage capacity. Moreover, it has been estimated that it would take a minimum of two years for the U.S. domestic energy supply to respond significantly to a cutoff of all oil imports from the Middle East.

Therefore, every country needs a plan for dealing with a supply interruption, based on an appropriate mix of fuel switching, stockpiles, and shut-in capacity. The magnitude of these precautions should be based on projected oil imports. The United States, Norway, Canada, and the United Kingdom can now, or soon will be able to, protect themselves in this way. But they cannot avoid the effects of the pressures that a general embargo would place on the other industrial nations without this capability. Trade with them would decline as their level of economic activity fell, and consequently, the exports of nations surviving the embargo would suffer, thus reducing their own economic activity. The present interdependence of the world economy does not permit any country to consider its economic welfare in isolation from that of its principal trading partners.

Their own national interests thus make it essential for countries with oil supplies to be prepared to make their supplies available to countries that lack supplies. The latter must, of course, assist in sharing the burden of any embargo by maintaining large stockpiles and by adopting energy-conservation measures during an emergency. Because stockpiles would be based on the volume of imported oil, the cost of these precautions would be greater for Europe and Japan, with their greater dependence on imports, than for Canada and the United States. By shouldering this greater cost, they would be sharing the burden as well as the benefits of an international emergency supply arrangement.

There is no basis for sharing that would be ideal for all countries. Nations that import most of their energy (like Japan) would be handicapped by a policy of prorating the total reduction in energy supplies to the industrial world. On the other hand, high-energy-consumption countries (like the United States) would be hurt by a policy based on equalizing per capita energy consumption.

International Energy Program. A program that does provide an acceptable basis for oil storage and sharing and also meets most of the other requirements for an effective emergency plan is the draft agreement among the eighteen member nations of the newly established International Energy Agency of OECD. The signatory governments are Austria, Belgium, Canada, Denmark, the Federal Republic of Germany, Ireland, Italy, Japan, Luxembourg, the Netherlands, New Zealand, Spain, Sweden, Switzerland, Turkey, the United Kingdom, and the United States. Norway is in effect a member, although there is some difference in the form of its membership. **We welcome the agreement on emergency oil storage and sharing among the countries in the International Energy Agency and urge its early ratification or approval by the signatory governments.**

The agency's mandate extends beyond contingency planning and includes cooperation in conservation and in the development of new energy sources. Its immediate thrust, however, results from the emergency oil-sharing plan. This plan binds its signatories to establish stockpiles equal to sixty days of oil-import requirements and to raise these supplies to ninety days in a few years. In the event of a selective or general embargo, they must automatically restrain oil consumption and share all available imported and indigenous oil supplies as certain supply-shortfall triggers are reached. For example, a reduction in supply to 93 percent of the previous year's level will trigger a 7 percent curtailment of consumption and a reallocation of available supplies to ensure that no country need reduce consumption more than others.

These emergency measures will go into effect automatically unless a strong majority of the participating countries votes to delay the operation of the trigger. There is thus a clear presumption of action in an emergency. The complex voting system is based essentially on countries' total oil consumption. An important feature is that unanimity is not required for decisions to be binding. We endorse the agreement because its ten-year life and virtually automatic character contribute much as an antidote for and deterrent to any oil-supply interruption.

It is important for importing countries to bear in mind that over the next few years, the oil-producing countries will themselves refine an increasing share of their crude oil output. Unless adequate excess refinery capacity is maintained in the consuming countries as a group, oil must be stockpiled in the form in which it is imported in order to replace those imports immediately in an emergency.

Not every industrial country is a signatory of this agreement. The agreement would be greatly enhanced if other OECD nations joined; the seriousness of all the OECD countries' intentions to deal firmly with supply interruptions would then be apparent. Moreover, with wide membership, the agreement on oil sharing in emergencies would serve more effectively as the basis for further long-term international cooperation in the energy field.

COOPERATION FOR CONSERVATION

Case for Conservation. Emergency energy conservation will be required in the event of an interruption in oil supplies. **To make the International Energy Agency program effective, each nation must maintain a continuously updated standby plan for emergency conservation and fuel allocation.** This plan should use whatever measures are most appropriate in each country.

Even without a new emergency, however, conservation is essential to each country's energy security and standard of living. If the recent growth rate of energy consumption is curbed, less oil will have to be imported, thus reducing the vulnerability of industrial countries to interruptions in their supplies and lessening the strain on their balance of payments. Over time, the world price of oil may even be reduced if the oil-consuming countries successfully conserve energy and lower their demand for imported oil. Although OPEC could maintain the price of oil in the face of reduced demand only by curbing its oil production, its willingness and ability to do this beyond a certain point is open to question. Such a move would require a degree of coordination of production that OPEC has not yet achieved.

Indeed, energy conservation should be an area in which the producing and consuming countries can cooperate. Petroleum is an exhaustible resource. Furthermore, it represents the only resource possessed by most of the Middle Eastern members of OPEC. They wish to use their oil revenues to finance their economic and social development so that they will achieve industrialization before their oil wealth is used up. At present consumption rates, Iran's oil supplies will run out in about thirty years. Iran, in particular, has argued that the oil-producing countries have an obligation to conserve their exhaustible reserves so that they will be available for such uses as the production of petrochemicals for which substitute materials are not readily available.

Conservation is important not just because of the reductions in energy consumption that it will achieve but also because of its positive effects on the environment and its psychological impact on the peoples of the industrial world. The world economy may be entering a period of scarcities and high prices for a number of primary materials. Conservation reinforces the awareness that efficiency is essential to the maintenance of economic and social well-being when resources are scarce.

International Actions for Conservation. The potential for reducing oil consumption by efficiency measures and changes in consumption patterns differs in each country. For example, Japan is much less able to save energy by increasing the miles per gallon of its automobile stock than the United States and Canada are. A formal international agreement to conserve energy by a common percentage is thus extremely unlikely. The only exception is in the case of an emergency, when equal conservation is the essential prerequisite to the sharing of available oil supplies. But if energy-conserving nations are not simply to release supplies to nonconserving nations, some sort of informal international understanding on conservation is essential. The obvious forum for such discussion is IEA, particularly if France should join. We thus welcome the fact that this new agency will be concerned with conservation as well as with other aspects of the energy problem.

Once the different national positions toward energy conservation are understood through discussions within IEA, it might attempt to establish nonbinding but indicative energy-consumption targets for each of its members. These targets would obviously be different for each country. However, their existence, especially if combined with a system of regular reporting on their attainment, would greatly reduce possible recrimination against and misunderstanding of those countries that are unable to conserve very much and would help to stiffen the resolve of those governments tempted to relax conservation programs.

We recommend that the International Energy Agency establish an international clearing system for information on techniques and economic policies for energy conservation. Existing techniques and policies and current areas of research should be included in order to stimulate creative interchange while avoiding unnecessary duplication.

Although the mutual exchange of existing information should facilitate conservation in all countries, more needs to be learned about possible efficiencies in the use of energy. Most countries are now committed to research to improve efficiency; however, an international division of conservation research and development efforts would achieve results at lower cost to each country. **We recommend that the International Energy Agency both establish and coordinate the most wide-ranging international program of conservation research possible.*** Internationally coordinated research into ways of utilizing the heat now wasted in the generation of electricity would be particularly useful.

National Policies for Conservation. Because most energy is consumed within national boundaries, almost all policies to conserve it will necessarily be national, utilizing the results of international information and research programs. Although the scope of this statement is limited to possibilities for international action, some brief comment about national policies is in order. Differences of climate, population density, industrial and economic structures, and living standards mean that countries will conserve energy in different ways and to different degrees. Our concern is that they make a vigorous effort to reduce consumption of oil.

Higher prices and the worldwide slowdown in economic activity reduced world oil consumption in 1974 far below past trends, but by the end of 1974, few countries had adopted strong and explicit energy conservation policies. France took the lead with its plan to limit expenditures on imported oil to fr. 51 billion in 1975, although the impact of this action was relieved by the strengthening of the franc in terms of the dollar and by general recessionary conditions. Other steps are appropriate to other countries. For example, in addition to expenditure limits, oil imports can be reduced directly through the imposition of tariffs or quantitative ceilings that are part of a comprehensive scheme of allocation and/or rationing. Among additional measures to discourage oil consumption are increased gasoline and fuel oil taxes; higher taxes or license fees on those automobiles, appliances, and other machines that use energy inefficiently; adoption and vigorous enforcement of lower speed limits; energy rate structures designed to discourage inefficient energy use; subsidies for such energy-saving measures as public transportation and home insulation.**

OECD countries should give higher priority to the development of comprehensive national conservation plans to restrain their own oil consumption and imports by whatever means are appropriate to their economies.

See memorandum by *JOHN SAGAN, page 95.
See memorandum by **JOHN SAGAN, page 96.

COOPERATION TO
DEVELOP NEW SOURCES OF SUPPLY

OPEC actions have already prompted national energy initiatives in various countries. Project Independence aims to reduce U.S. dependence on imported energy by increasing the supply of domestic oil and gas from both old and new wells, by more efficiently developing vast domestic coal reserves and using coal gasification, by producing oil from oil shale, and by accelerating utilization of nuclear power and research into unconventional sources such as geothermal and solar energy. The United States certainly has the reserves to enable it to become substantially self-sufficient in energy by 1985.

Few other countries are so fortunately endowed. In Europe, only the United Kingdom and Norway enjoy the possibility of self-sufficiency because of North Sea gas and oil. However, the United Kingdom and Germany have considerable domestic coal reserves to develop. France has embarked on a program of massive investment in nuclear power plants and in offshore exploration. All European countries are conducting research into future sources of energy, and some of this research is being undertaken on an international basis. The Common Market has passed a resolution calling for a common energy policy, but this has yet to take final shape. Whatever steps are taken, however, Europe does not appear to have the capacity to become self-sufficient in energy for a very long time.

Neither will Japan be able to avoid continued reliance on imported energy. Its Sunshine Project, which seeks to lessen this reliance, calls for expanded nuclear capacity and a revival of the domestic coal industry. The project also includes research to provide for Japan's energy needs in the more distant future.

A serious problem in stimulating the development of new indigenous energy supplies in the OECD countries is that of providing adequate incentives to potential investors. The main impetus to the development of new energy supplies has come from the higher world price of oil. There is consensus that a world oil price of $10 a barrel in 1974 dollars is adequate to ensure the development of substantial new sources of supply. But the future course of oil prices is highly uncertain for a variety of reasons, including the fact that the present price of imported oil bears no relation to the cost of its production. This uncertainty could, in time, act as a major deterrent to the large-scale investment in new supplies that is needed if the goal of energy security is to be achieved.

The problem is compounded because the likelihood of realizing lower prices for imported oil is increased to the extent that programs of conservation and development of domestic energy resources are vigorously pursued by OECD countries. At the same time, the expectation of lower real prices could lead to the contraction or cancellation of precisely those domestic energy investment plans on which the expectation of reduced prices is based.

*What is needed is some form of national guarantee to investors in expensive new energy sources. The guarantee should be primarily directed to investment in high-cost unconventional fuels such as synthetics and shale. In particular cases, special incentives may also be needed for investment in conventional fuels. However, we see no present need for a common floor price for petroleum; in fact, we believe it could even strengthen OPEC's ability to keep prices up. The nature of the guarantee for high-cost energy investment is a matter of national policy, and we tend to favor a case-by-case approach.**

From the point of view of the world economy, the development of higher-cost indigenous energy in the OECD countries represents an economic waste in the face of the vast (but not unlimited) supplies of oil available in the Middle East at low real costs in terms of capital and labor. But this is a price that must be paid for security of supply and protection against exorbitant price demands on the part of the oil cartel.

These matters should be addressed now because national energy plans are still being drawn up and international cooperation can be more easily incorporated into them at present than will be possible in the future. A number of specific areas for cooperation are discussed in the following paragraphs.

Oil. It is generally agreed that the onshore prospects of exploiting significant additional volumes of conventional crude oil in the OECD countries are negligible in the near future except in the United States (Alaska) and Canada. If tax policy is conducive, current estimates of future world prices of oil should provide oil companies with adequate incentives to develop North American supplies even when the extra costs that will result from meeting environmental controls and from improving recovery operations to increase well productivity are taken into account.

Offshore oil, particularly from the North Sea and off the American coasts, probably represents the most promising near-term approach to meeting our energy needs.

See memorandum by *ELVIS J. STAHR, page 95.

Nuclear Energy. An increase in the proportion of total energy needs to be met by nuclear power is called for in the energy plans of most countries. The attractions of nuclear energy are considerable. Unlike other fuels, uranium ore is not concentrated in any particular region of the world; rather, it is widely distributed. Furthermore, it is easy to transport and store. In the more distant future, breeder reactors and possibly fusion offer the prospect of inexhaustible sources of energy. And although nuclear power involves many controversial and unresolved issues, a number of these are particularly amenable to solution through international cooperation.

Most reactors presently in operation or planned for the immediate future require enriched uranium as fuel. There has been concern that there will be neither sufficient uranium ore nor adequate enrichment facilities to meet the needs of the new reactors. Rationalizing the world's enriched uranium situation will be difficult. It is complicated by the very considerable political factors such as the possible diversion of nuclear fuels to military uses and the dissemination of classified information. Nevertheless, adequate uranium supplies and enrichment facilities are essential. *We welcome the announcement that the International Energy Agency will concern itself with the problem of ensuring adequate supplies of enriched uranium and urge it to do so quickly.**

Coal. Australia, Canada, and the United States have coal reserves far in excess of their domestic needs. Indeed, it has been estimated that U.S. coal reserves are sufficient to supply the world's total energy needs for almost a century, even at greatly increased rates of production. Coal production has been rising in recent years in the United States,** but it has been declining in Europe and Japan. Although the increased price of oil serves as a major incentive to halt this decline, the European and Japanese coal industries have a limited capacity for expansion compared with that of the United States and Australia. However, Europe and Japan will be able to take advantage of North American and Australian coal only within the framework of liberal coal-import and -export policies.

The greatest scope for international cooperation to produce and use coal lies in research and development. To help the immediate situation, internationally coordinated research and exchange of information are needed on ways to improve coal mining techniques and transportation technologies, to increase the capability for reclamation of surface-mined land, and to find cleaner ways to burn coal in power stations. We note

See memorandum by *ELVIS J. STAHR, page 96.
See memorandum by **R. HEATH LARRY, page 97.

that Japanese experience in cleaning emissions from power plant stacks may well prove helpful to other countries.

Coal would be a cleaner and more useful fuel if it were gasified or liquefied because the polluting elements in coal, particularly sulfur, are removed during processing. Moreover, synthetic gas or oil from coal could be transported in existing pipelines. Coal gasification processes are more advanced than methods of liquefaction, and a number of gasification processes are now in advanced stages of development.

Research. * The amount of energy research required is enormous. No one country can possibly allocate resources sufficient to cover all needed energy research. International cooperation in research should therefore produce results more efficiently than strictly national efforts. Furthermore, certain countries already have a comparative advantage in particular areas (e.g., Canada in tar sands and France and Britain in fast breeder reactors).

We welcome IEA's inclusion of research within its mandate and suggest that particular areas ripe for international cooperation in this or other forums include improved techniques for coal mining, reclamation of surface-mined land, cleaner burning of coal in power stations, and economically feasible coal gasification and liquefaction. For the longer term, research on solar energy, the extraction of energy from refuse, geothermal energy, and nuclear fusion should be coordinated internationally.*

BROADER COOPERATION BETWEEN
CONSUMING AND PRODUCING COUNTRIES

Much has been made recently of the need to avoid confrontation between the producers and the importers of oil. We agree. Indeed, there is considerable identity of interests between the two groups. The producers quite legitimately wish to develop their countries; the importers need oil if their industrial societies are not to be brought to a halt. The industrial countries should thus make technical and managerial skills available to the oil producers to assist their development and reduce their dependence on a depleting resource. At the same time, however, they must cooperate among themselves in order to balance the newly gained bargaining strength of the producers.

The measures of cooperation among consuming countries that we have endorsed include support from central banks for Eurobanks facing

See memoranda by *ELVIS J. STAHR, page 95.

liquidity problems because of abrupt shifts of funds; the safety-net facility, through which consuming countries provide mutual financial support while reinforcing their economic cooperation; closer cooperation
between IMF and GATT in the surveillance of trade restrictions for balance-of-payments reasons; emergency sharing of petroleum supplies;
and more urgent steps to conserve energy and develop new sources of
production.

Collaboration among the oil consumers is an essential condition for
any broader cooperation between producing and consuming countries.
One area in which this wider cooperation could be particularly fruitful
is in the use of OPEC capital to help finance the development of new
energy sources, particularly to provide for the time when world oil
reserves are exhausted.

In addition, we have recommended that such cooperation take the
form of a new OPEC-OECD credit facility to assist countries hard pressed
to pay their oil-import bills and a series of joint measures to assist developing countries. Although the time is not yet ripe for a commodity agreement on oil, we have endorsed a more positive approach toward commodity agreements on other primary materials and toward the local
processing of energy and raw materials by OPEC members and other
developing countries. We have also endorsed enlarged financial support
for the most severely affected developing countries through the interest-
subsidy feature of the IMF oil facility, larger contributions to IDA (the
soft-loan facility of the World Bank), and the establishment of a "third
window" at the World Bank. These mechanisms should help to reinforce
a triangular relationship in which OPEC countries channel part of their
surpluses to the poor countries, which, in turn, use them to import from
the industrial countries those goods and services essential to their development. At the same time, this triangulation permits the OECD countries to
pay *currently* for a larger fraction of their oil imports by means of additional exports to the developing countries.

Memoranda of
Comment, Reservation,
or Dissent

Page 11, by THEODORE O. YNTEMA, *with which* GILBERT E. JONES, JOHN A. PERKINS, *and* C. WREDE PETERSMEYER *have asked to be associated*

This statement, as well as the preceding one on energy policy, is based on a fallacious assumption: that our major objective should be to reduce the price of oil. Such reduction would ease some near-term problems, but in the long run, it would be disastrous. Instead, our objective—certainly in the long run—should be to have the prices of oil and gas high enough to conserve these precious resources and high enough to speed the changeover to major reliance on nuclear reactions and coal (also sunlight and perhaps tar sands and shale) as sources of energy. For us in the United States, the leading nation in the free world, there is an overriding consideration: We cannot have economic or even real political independence unless we can get along without OPEC oil. And we will not take the actions to develop enough substitute sources of energy unless the prices of oil and gas are, and will remain, high enough to make such actions attractive.

Most of the recommendations in this statement seem to me desirable, although many are probably of doubtful feasibility. What I miss is a focus on the main goal: rapid development of substitute sources of energy. We can and will survive high-priced oil, and someday, we shall recognize that OPEC did us a favor by acting as soon as it did. We shall be in deep trouble if the price of oil fluctuates by large amounts. And if the price of oil comes down by much, we shall probably remain under the thumb of the Middle East oil countries for a long time to come.

Page 13, by R. HEATH LARRY

I doubt that the primary objective of conservation and development of alternate supplies is to "lower the world price of oil," as indicated. The major objective is probably to assure availability of adequate energy supplies.

90

Page 13, by R. HEATH LARRY

Perhaps because I have read so much about the energy problem, my impression of this statement is that it is out of date. Had it been published in the third quarter of 1974, it would have done a good job of summarizing contemporary thoughts and opinions being expressed at that time. For example, it considers (1) the possible sizable buildup in OPEC surpluses, (2) the problem of recycling OPEC excess funds through the private-sector banking system or through special monetary funds, (3) the need for direct negotiations among oil-producing and -consuming nations, and (4) the need for cooperation among oil-consuming nations with regard to saving energy, sharing energy, storing energy, and stimulating alternate sources. All these things have been discussed time and again. Some progress has been, and is being, made toward solution of these problems. Current thinking, as noted briefly in the statement, indicates OPEC surpluses may not be so large as originally forecast. In summary, there is little in this statement that has not been covered more than adequately by other reports and articles of this nature. For this reason, I question the need for or desirability of attempting to insert specific reservations or comments.

Several sections of the report deal with the problem of providing funds to developing nations so that they can pay for the energy they must consume. At no place does the report discuss or even give recognition to the fact that the schemes suggested for supporting developing nations do little more than keep them from complete financial collapse. The suggestion is made that funds be provided "in amounts sufficient to enable the poorest countries to sustain acceptable rates of growth." This is a commendable objective, but no one has yet specified how funds would be used to realize this objective or provided any estimate of the magnitude of the funds required. I cannot help but believe that the amounts required might be beyond the capabilities of developed nations. This factor has led to some of the harsh current thinking regarding a "lifeboat" theory.

The primary thrust of this report is to recommend strengthening functions of international agencies such as GATT, OECD, and so forth. In particular, OECD is suggested as the agency which should play a key role in evolving negotiations between producer and consumer countries. In the first instance, as suggested here, such agencies are information-gathering bodies. Next, they become responsible for establishment of "guidelines." The next step, which is not articulated, probably means controls, sanctions, and so forth. For example, one recommendation calls for OECD "to develop guidelines for treatment of foreign official investments in the light of the new situation, keeping in mind the ultimate objective of securing an open world market for capital." The concept of guidelines and open markets seems somewhat incompatible.

The report discusses the need for and possibility of a world commodity agreement on oil that would include provisions on price, supply, and other factors. This is mentioned in the summary on page 32 and is more fully developed in the body of the report on pages 72 and 73. However, the conclusion is reached that indexing is not an appropriate principle for setting the price of oil. This judgment does not flow from the discussion presented, since indexing is never mentioned as a possible pricing mechanism.

Page 13, by G. BARRON MALLORY

Although I approve of the statement in general, I feel obliged to present strong reservations to portions thereof. These comments are inspired by the interests of the United States, particularly in view of OPEC's proposed further increases in oil prices after September 30, 1975. Secretary of the Treasury William Simon recently stated that the OPEC prices generally are related, not to economic reality, but rather to political considerations. These considerations are generally inimical to interests of the OECD countries.

While the statement is not a full admission of defeat by the OECD countries, it is replete with offers by them of concessions to OPEC, presupposing a great deal of community interest between the exporters and importers. Of course, neither group wants to precipitate a world crisis arising from a continuing worldwide recession and further inflation, but the community of interest stops about there.

It is true that there are varying degrees of vulnerability to oil prices and consequent payments deficits among the countries making up OECD (the United States being one of the least vulnerable), yet there is a great deal of conflict of interest within OPEC. The countries bordering on the Arabian Gulf have one kind of objective which is inconsistent with the interests of those on the Mediterranean. The producers in the Northern and Southern Hemispheres have different goals, and within each region, the different countries frequently have antagonistic national interests to promote. Some wish to reduce the production of oil to keep prices up, and others are more interested in receiving revenue even at lower prices. The quality of the crude in one area varies from that in another, and the distance and means of delivery to the consumers are different. It is well known that among the OPEC members various devices are used to hide price concessions to consuming countries.

Instead of proposing weak-kneed accommodations by OECD, it would seem more logical for OECD to let it be well known that it recognizes the dissensions within OPEC stemming from the great diversity of interests among its members.

Various attempts in the statement to further cooperation between producers and consumers seem so impractical and unworkable as to be Pollyannaish. Examples of such attempts are set forth in my comment on page 93.

Page 13, by JAMES Q. RIORDAN

In my judgment, the policy statement has focused to a disproportionate degree upon the area of international agreements. New international agreements will be very difficult to reach and cannot be counted on to solve our energy problems. While the statement recognizes these difficulties, I nonetheless sense a degree of optimism that, in my judgment, may not be warranted.

The policy statement does not sufficiently emphasize the need to increase energy investments. All the basic steps that can be taken to increase non-OPEC energy supplies and to conserve energy will require major capital investments. These investments will have to be made largely by the private sector, which, in turn, will require a stable and consistent climate if it is to attract the capital needed. In many countries, governments will need to eliminate counterproductive controls and taxation if the needed investments are to be made.

Page 14, by R. HEATH LARRY

To illustrate the increase in the world price of crude petroleum, this figure shows posted prices in the Middle East. The footnote does explain the problem of using posted prices as a basis for illustrating the real price of oil, but the reader must make his own interpretation. It would seem that a better indicator of world oil prices might be available.

Page 19, by R. HEATH LARRY

This section seems to overstress the role of increased oil prices as a cause of world inflation. Subsequently (on page 65), it is admitted that most of the inflationary pressure came from within the OECD area itself and that increased oil prices accentuated the inflationary problems already inherent in most of the world's economies.

Pages 27 and 56, by FRAZAR B. WILDE

It will be more effective, and we will reach a quicker solution, if we have an agreement to use Special Drawing Rights or some other combined currency value for oil payments. The present situation is very unworkable and undesirable.

Pages 29 and 63, by G. BARRON MALLORY

The suggestion that the countries within the two groups work out "equitably" contributions to IMF and IDA does not warrant much credence. As suggested on pages 55 and 56, the investment by the OPEC countries of their excess funds is a real problem. However, to hand them a list of potential investments in the OECD countries or to create special OECD government bonds for this purpose seems politically unfeasible and repugnant to the individual countries. On page 27, the phrase "reciprocity rule" appears. OPEC nationalizes oil investments of foreign corporations, but it is unthinkable for OECD to reciprocate. It is futile to think that the OPEC countries will be willing to invest funds to help the consuming countries through loans and other investments to reduce reliance upon petroleum products as suggested on page 89.

It is suggested that while it is obviously necessary for OECD to deal with the producer cartel, there is a danger of further concessions to OPEC in that these would encourage other unilateral cartels among producers of other raw materials and commodities which are necessary to the consuming nations. Such unilateral cartels are already in the making (Paris meeting in April), and unfortunately, Secretary of State Kissinger indicated in May that the United States might consider such arrangements.

Pages 30 and 68, by HERMAN L. WEISS, *with which* JAMES Q. RIORDAN *has asked to be associated*

International trade is already encumbered with an excess of restrictions, and it is difficult to visualize how additional restrictions on a discriminatory basis would be helpful. GATT is a statement of general rules which on too many occasions have been violated by contracting parties. The adoption of amendments to GATT and IMF articles to allow the use of "appropriate" measures in addition to quotas would only aggravate the existing situation.

Pages 32 and 71, by HERMAN L. WEISS, *with which* JAMES Q. RIORDAN *has asked to be associated.*

Encouraging international commodity agreements does not appear to be a feasible way of ordering world trade. Negotiating such agreements would be long and arduous, and conditions could be entirely different by the time such agreements could be consummated.

Page 34, by HERMAN L. WEISS, *with which* JAMES Q. RIORDAN *has asked to be associated*

This section places primary emphasis on the conservation of energy, principally oil, but gives little attention to the development of new energy supplies. Higher-priced energy will, through market forces, encourage greater efficiency in all types of usage and the design of more energy efficient products and facilities. This, plus other conservation programs, will cause the consumption of energy per unit of output to decline. However, since energy consumption per unit of output will eventually approach some lower limit, total energy supplies must be increased to support continued economic growth. High priority should be assigned to immediate development of energy supplies because lead times are long, investment requirements are large, and governments must be involved, frequently in cooperative efforts with industry.

Pages 35 and 84, by JOHN SAGAN

In my opinion, it is a mistake to expect the International Energy Agency to establish energy-consumption targets for each of its members. Each member country has its own more or less unique circumstance reflecting conditions of geography, climate, land usage, type of economic activity, and so forth. Even if a reasonable method could be devised to account for these factors and to establish meaningful targets, the wide differences among the targets could lead to much misunderstanding. Moreover, little would be gained by the process. The work of IEA is more likely to require projections of storage capacity and energy-production capability by country than consumption targets.

Pages 36 and 88, by ELVIS J. STAHR

The most urgently needed research is research on foolproof disposal of radioactive wastes, since no such system presently exists. Unless it is found, ensuring adequate supplies of enriched uranium is of very questionable priority.

Pages 36 and 88, by ELVIS J. STAHR

This list omits a very urgently needed area of research: namely, research in the storage of electricity. It is lack of storage capability which contributes perhaps more than anything to the economic problems of greatly increased use of solar energy, wind energy, and energy from the oceans (temperature gradients, wave action, and so forth) and even to conventional energy costs. Incidentally, the last-mentioned new energy sources (sun, winds, and oceans) might well be added to the list of fruitful and appropriate areas for international cooperative research efforts.

Pages 36 and 86, by ELVIS J. STAHR

Thus far, there is so much evidence that extracting oil from shale requires a high proportion of the amount of energy extracted and that the environmental consequences of shale exploitation are very grave that substantial shale development, before infinitely more research is done, would not be prudent, economically sound, or ecologically sane.

Page 60, by R. HEATH LARRY

In reviewing the causes of the substantial rise in commodity prices in the 1972–1974 period, the factor of speculation has been omitted.

Page 67, by R. HEATH LARRY

In discussing the fact that trade measures such as quota restrictions and import surcharges should not be used to protect a nation's balance of payments, the statement fails to recognize that some economies may be forced to use such measures as a purely defensive retaliation against the impact of subsidies and other forms of export stimulation.

Page 84, by JOHN SAGAN

I am reluctant to accept the view that governmental actions such as tariffs, quantitative ceilings, differential license fees, or other artificial restrictions should be imposed in order to reduce the consumption of petroleum. My concern has several aspects: First, I believe that market forces working through the pricing mechanism can do a far better job of petroleum allocation than any government agency, no matter how wise or well intended. Second, government intervention might be justified during a period of emergency but would become counterproductive if sustained for a very long period of time. Third, it is probable that artificial restrictions on consumption would actually work to retard the energy-supply increases which would otherwise result if the price mechanism were allowed to function.

I believe that a policy designed to create and manage a shortage is likely to perpetuate that shortage; whereas the market itself could balance supply and demand quickly and efficiently.

Page 87, by ELVIS J. STAHR

A good many people, of whom I am one, are having second thoughts about the wisdom of accelerating efforts to solve energy problems through widespread use of nuclear energy. The reasons for doubt are various and unfortunately numerous, and some of them are of such seriousness that they deserve a great deal more consideration than they have received in this policy statement. Nuclear energy should never be lumped in with other energy sources, as if all were useful to exploit to the limit of capability, because nuclear energy is *different* in some profoundly important ways.

Page 87, by R. HEATH LARRY

The report says, "Coal production has been rising in recent years in the United States." If "recent years" is taken to mean a period of a decade, this is probably true; but in the last five years, bituminous coal production has simply not increased beyond the 603-million-ton level achieved in 1970.

A.

APPENDIX A: IMPORTS OF PETROLEUM AND OTHER PRIMARY PRODUCTS, BY SELECTED
INDUSTRIAL COUNTRIES, 1969, 1973, AND 1974

	Millions of U.S. Dollars			Percent of Total Imports		
	1969	1973	1974	1969	1973	1974
UNITED STATES TOTAL IMPORTS	36,052	69,476	100,972	100.0	100.0	100.0
Food	5,309	9,239	10,701	14.7	13.3	10.6
Raw Materials	3,595	5,269	6,459	9.9	7.6	6.4
Ores, Other Minerals	1,313	2,123	2,862	3.6	3.1	2.8
Agricultural	2,282	3,146	3,597	6.3	4.5	3.6
Mineral Fuels	2,794	8,174	25,340	7.7	11.8	25.1
Petroleum	2,560	7,614	24,200	7.1	11.0	24.0
Others	234	560	1,140	0.6	0.8	1.1
JAPAN TOTAL IMPORTS	15,024	38,134	62,076	100.0	100.0	100.0
Food	2,141	5,973	8,134	14.3	15.7	13.1
Raw Materials	5,401	12,199	14,285	35.9	32.0	23.0
Ores, Other Minerals	2,220	4,436	5,335	14.7	11.6	8.6
Agricultural	3,181	7,763	8,950	21.2	20.4	14.4
Mineral Fuels	3,044	8,305	24,849	20.3	21.8	40.0
Petroleum	2,298	6,710	21,156	15.3	17.6	34.1
Others	746	1,595	3,693	5.0	4.2	5.9
AUSTRALIA TOTAL IMPORTS	4,004	6,813	11,148	100.0	100.0	100.0
Food	200	343	547	5.0	5.0	4.9
Raw Materials	275	516	713	6.9	7.6	6.4
Ores, Other Minerals	73	102	—	1.8	1.5	—
Agricultural	202	414	—	5.0	6.1	—
Mineral Fuels	296	279	935	7.4	4.1	8.4
Petroleum	295	278	—	7.4	4.1	—
Others	1	1	—	0.0	0.0	—

	%	%	%	Value	Value	Value
Food	8.8	12.4	13.3	4,673	4,557	2,295
Raw Materials	10.2	10.4	11.6	5,368	3,843	2,058
Ores, Other Minerals	—	2.2	2.4	—	823	476
Agricultural	—	8.2	9.2	—	3,020	1,582
Mineral Fuels	22.4	12.4	11.4	11,807	4,546	1,965
Petroleum	—	10.4	9.2	—	3,839	1,592
Others	—	2.0	2.2	—	707	373
GERMANY TOTAL IMPORTS	100.0	100.0	100.0	69,645	54,496	24,926
Food	13.1	16.5	17.4	9,114	9,003	4,332
Raw Materials	12.2	11.9	14.5	8,554	6,490	3,618
Ores, Other Minerals	4.3	3.8	5.3	3,027	2,073	1,332
Agricultural	7.9	8.1	9.2	5,527	4,417	2,286
Mineral Fuels	19.1	11.4	8.9	13,302	6,211	2,208
Petroleum	17.9	10.4	8.1	12,480	5,703	2,021
Others	1.2	1.0	0.8	822	508	187
ITALY TOTAL IMPORTS	100.0a	100.0	100.0	40,968a	27,846	12,450
Food	14.3	20.1	17.8	5,875	5,607	2,218
Raw Materials	15.5	16.3	18.9	6,346	4,528	2,353
Ores, Other Minerals	—	3.7	4.7	—	1,033	589
Agricultural	—	12.6	14.2	—	3,495	1,764
Mineral Fuels	25.9	14.1	14.6	10,631	3,925	1,815
Petroleum	—	13.0	13.2	—	3,612	1,647
Others	—	1.1	1.4	—	313	168
UNITED KINGDOM TOTAL IMPORTS	100.0	100.0	100.0	54,228	38,875	19,956
Food	16.3	19.5	23.3	8,856	7,596	4,642
Raw Materials	11.2	12.4	15.1	6,053	4,818	3,010
Ores, Other Minerals	3.0	3.0	4.3	1,580	1,153	850
Agricultural	8.2	9.4	10.8	4,473	3,665	2,160
Mineral Fuels	20.2	10.9	10.9	10,937	4,235	2,184
Petroleum	19.6	10.6	10.7	10,617	4,124	2,135
Others	0.6	0.3	0.2	320	111	49

(continued)

APPENDIX A: IMPORTS OF PETROLEUM AND OTHER PRIMARY PRODUCTS, BY SELECTED
INDUSTRIAL COUNTRIES, 1969, 1973, AND 1974   (continued)

A.

	Millions of U.S. Dollars			Percent of Total Imports		
	1969	1973	1974	1969	1973	1974
SWEDEN TOTAL IMPORTS	5,899	10,543	15,744	100.0	100.0	100.0
Food	595	994	1,162	10.1	9.4	7.4
Raw Materials	365	528	764	6.2	5.0	4.9
Ores, Other Minerals	158	196	—	2.7	1.9	—
Agricultural	207	332	—	3.5	3.2	—
Mineral Fuels	621	1,202	2,831	10.5	11.4	18.0
Petroleum	546	1,072	—	9.3	10.2	—
Others	75	130	—	1.3	1.2	—
TOTAL, ABOVE COUNTRIES						
TOTAL IMPORTS	135,531	282,946	407,605	100.0	100.0	100.0
Food	21,732	43,312	49,062	16.1	15.3	12.0
Raw Materials	20,675	38,191	48,542	15.3	13.5	11.9
Ores, Other Minerals	7,011	11,939	—	5.2	4.2	—
Agricultural	13,664	26,252	—	10.1	9.3	—
Mineral Fuels	14,927	36,877	100,632	11.0	13.0	24.7
Petroleum	13,093	32,952	—	9.7	11.6	—
Others	1,833	3,925	—	1.4	1.4	—

a Data for Italy are based on the first three quarters of 1974.
SOURCES: OECD, *Statistics of Foreign Trade, Trade by Commodities*; UN, *Commodity Trade Statistics*; and national sources.

APPENDIX B: DAILY WORLD CRUDE OIL PRODUCTION, 1960, 1970, 1973, AND 1974

Area and Country	Thousand of Barrels				Percent Distribution				
	1960	1970	1973	1974	1960	1970	1973	1974	
WESTERN HEMISPHERE	11,315	16,131	16,118	15,390	53.8	36.0	29.0	28.0	
United States	7,055	9,648	9,189	8,890	33.6	21.3	16.5	16.0	
Canada	519	1,305	1,798	1,720	2.5	2.4	3.2	3.1	
Venezuela	2,845	3,703	3,364	2,970	13.5	8.2	6.1	5.3	
Others	896	1,475	1,767	1,810	4.3	3.3	3.2	3.2	
WESTERN EUROPE	289	375	370	390	1.4	0.8	0.7	0.7	
MIDDLE EAST	5,269	13,937	21,158	21,710	25.1	30.7	38.0	38.9	
Saudi Arabia	1,319	3,798	7,607	8,480	6.3	8.4	13.7	15.2	
Iran	1,057	3,831	5,861	6,040	5.0	8.4	10.5	10.8	
Kuwait	1,696	2,983	3,024	2,550	8.1	6.6	5.4	4.6	
Iraq	969	1,563	1,964	1,780	4.6	3.5	3.5	3.2	
Abu Dhabi	0	691	1,298	1,410	—	2.0	2.3	2.5	
Others	228	1,071	1,404	1,450	1.1	2.4	2.5	2.6	
AFRICA	289	5,982	5,902	5,330	1.4	13.2	10.6	9.6	
Libya	0	3,321	2,187	1,500	—	7.3	4.0	2.7	
Nigeria	18	1,090	2,053	2,270	0.1	2.4	3.7	4.1	
Algeria	185	976	1,070	940	0.9	2.2	1.9	1.7	
Others	86	595	592	620	0.4	1.3	1.1	1.1	

(continued)

APPENDIX B: DAILY WORLD CRUDE OIL PRODUCTION, 1960, 1970, 1973, AND 1974 *(continued)*

Area and Country	Thousand of Barrels				Percent Distribution			
	1960	1970	1973	1974	1960	1970	1973	1974
ASIA-PACIFIC	554	1,340	2,272	2,300	2.6	3.0	4.1	4.1
Indonesia	419	855	1,339	1,360	2.0	1.9	2.4	2.4
Others	135	485	933	940	0.6	1.1	1.7	1.7
COMMUNIST COUNTRIES	3,310	7,610	9,865	10,650	15.7	16.8	17.7	19.1
Soviet Union	2,960	7,049	8,420	8,950	14.1	15.5	15.1	16.1
Eastern Europe, China	350	561	1,445	1,700	1.7	1.2	2.6	3.1
WORLD TOTAL	21,026	45,375	55,685	55,770	100.0	100.0	100.0	100.0

SOURCE: U.S. Council on International Economic Policy, *International Economic Report of the President* (Washington, D.C.: U.S. Government Printing Office, 1975).

APPENDIX C: WORLD PRIMARY ENERGY CONSUMPTION, 1974

Area and Country	Million Tons of Oil Equivalent						Percent of World Total
	Oil	Natural Gas	Solid Fuels	Water Power	Nuclear	Total	
WESTERN HEMISPHERE	1,052.4	672.5	360.9	167.6	34.0	2,287.4	37.7
United States	785.4	560.4	331.9	76.9	28.8	1,783.4	29.4
Canada	88.1	64.1	15.0	59.4	4.9	231.5	3.8
Others	178.9	48.0	14.0	31.3	0.3	272.5	4.5
WESTERN EUROPE	699.2	146.1	261.9	100.3	18.5	1,226.0	20.2
European Community of Six[a]	418.1	107.9	134.0	28.7	7.4	696.1	11.5
United Kingdom	105.8	30.8	68.9	1.3	7.3	214.1	3.5
Others	175.3	7.4	59.0	70.3	3.8	315.8	5.2
EASTERN HEMISPHERE[b]	991.3	315.7	1,145.4	96.4	9.4	2,558.2	42.1
Japan	261.1	5.1	58.8	19.0	4.1	348.1	5.7
Australasia	33.9	4.1	26.1	2.4	—	66.5	1.1
Soviet Union, Eastern Europe, China[c]	468.9	264.5	925.7	53.9	4.3	1,717.3	28.3
Others	227.4	42.0	134.8	21.1	1.0	426.3	7.0
WORLD TOTAL	2,742.9	1,134.3	1,768.2	364.3	61.9	6,071.6	100.0
FREE WORLD TOTAL[d]	2,274.0	869.8	842.5	310.4	57.6	4,354.3	—

a Belgium, France, Italy, Luxembourg, Netherlands, and West Germany.
b Excluding Western Europe.
c Including Albania, North Korea, and North Vietnam.
d World total excluding Eastern Europe, China, and Soviet Union.
SOURCE: *Statistical Review of the World Oil Industry, 1974* (London: British Petroleum Company, 1975).

Objectives of the Committee for Economic Development

For three decades, the Committee for Economic Development has had a respected influence on business and public policy. Composed of two hundred leading business executives and educators, CED is devoted to these two objectives:

To develop, through objective research and informed discussion, findings and recommendations for private and public policy which will contribute to preserving and strengthening our free society, achieving steady economic growth at high employment and reasonably stable prices, increasing productivity and living standards, providing greater and more equal opportunity for every citizen, and improving the quality of life for all.

To bring about increasing understanding by present and future leaders in business, government, and education and among concerned citizens of the importance of these objectives and the ways in which they can be achieved.

CED's work is supported strictly by private voluntary contributions from business and industry, foundations, and individuals. It is independent, nonprofit, nonpartisan, and nonpolitical.

The two hundred trustees, who generally are presidents or board chairmen of corporations and presidents of universities, are chosen for their individual capacities rather than as representatives of any particular interests. By working with scholars, they unite business judgment and experience with scholarship in analyzing the issues and developing recommendations to resolve the economic problems that constantly arise in a dynamic and democratic society.

Through this business-academic partnership, CED endeavors to develop policy statements and other research materials that commend themselves as guides to public and business policy; for use as texts in college economics and political science courses and in management training courses; for consideration and discussion by newspaper and magazine editors, columnists, and commentators; and for distribution abroad to promote better understanding of the American economic system.

CED believes that by enabling businessmen to demonstrate constructively their concern for the general welfare, it is helping business to earn and maintain the national and community respect essential to the successful functioning of the free enterprise capitalist system.

Honorary Trustees

CEPES: European Committee for Economic and Social Progress (Germany)

IDEP: Institut de l'Entreprise (France)

President
JEAN CHENEVIER
Président Directeur Général de la
Société Française des Pétroles BP

GEORGES ROBERT
Président de la Compagnie Française du Méthane

PIERRE DESPRAIRIES
Directeur de l'Institut du Pétrole

GEORGES GUERON
Vice-Président Directeur Général de la
Société Internationale des Conseillers de
Synthèse

PEP: Political and Economic Planning (Britain)

Executive Committee of PEP[1]

Chairman
SIR MONTAGUE FINNISTON, FRS.
Chairman, British Steel Corporation

Hon. Treasurer
PETER PARKER, MVO
Chairman, Rockware Group

Members
DR. MARK ABRAMS
Director, Social Science Research
Council, Survey Unit

SIR DENIS BARNES, Chairman
Manpower Services Commission

SIR HERMAN BONDI, KCB. FRS. FRAS
Chief Scientific Adviser
Ministry of Defence

PROFESSOR ASA BRIGGS
Vice-Chancellor
University of Sussex

J. C. BURGH
Deputy Secretary
Department of Prices and Consumer Protection

THE RT. HON. LORD BYERS, PC. OBE
Chairman
Companies Pensions Information Centre

PROFESSOR MICHEL CROZIER
Centre Nationale de la
Recherche Scientifique

MRS. JEAN FLOUD
Principal
Newnham College, Cambridge

DR. F. E. JONES
Executive Director
Phillips Industries

HECTOR LAING
Chairman
United Biscuits

SIR RONALD McINTOSH, KCB
Director-General
National Economic Development Office

PROFESSOR SIR CLAUS MOSER,
 KCB. CBE. EBA
Director
Central Statistical Office

JOHN E. NASH
Director of Monetary Affairs
Commission of the European Communities

J. A. PEEL, CBE. DL
Director of Industrial Relations
Commission of the European Communities

W. G. L. PLOWDEN
Under-Secretary
Central Policy Review Staff
Cabinet Office

GILES RADICE, M.P.
Labour Member of Parliament

W. G. RUNCIMAN
Director
Walter Runciman & Co.

THE LORD SAINSBURY
Joint-President
J. Sainsbury Ltd.

CHRISTOPHER TUGENDHAT M.P.
Conservative Member of Parliament

C. H. URWIN
Asst. General Secretary
Transport and General Workers Union

Director, PEP
JOHN PINDER

[1]The PEP Executive Committee authorized participation of four representatives of PEP in the preparation of this study. In keeping with PEP's normal procedures, it is not PEP as such but this group who join in taking responsibility for the study's content.

CEDA: Committee for Economic Development of Australia

Energy Study Committee

J. H. K. BRUNNER
Chief Economist
The Broken Hill Proprietary Co. Limited

R. CHAPMAN
State Electricity Commission of Victoria

T. D. CREGAN
Manager — Finance & Control
Cummins Diesel Australia

K. C. GALE
Managing Director
Gollin & Company Limited

V. McD. GIBSON
Chairman and Managing Director
Gibson Chemical Industries Limited

D. M. HOCKING
Economics Manager
Central Planning and Economics
The Shell Company of Australia Limited

P. S. PARKIN
Director
Mobil Oil Australia Limited

Ex Officio Members

D. H. MERRY
President
Committee for Economic Development
of Australia

PETER GREY
Executive Director
Committee for Economic Development
of Australia

Advisors

PROFESSOR J. W. NEVILLE
Head, School of Economics
University of New South Wales

PROFESSOR J. R. WILSON
Associate Professor of Economics
The University of Sydney

SNS: Industrial Council for Social and Economic Studies Sweden[2]

TORSTEN CARLSSON
Senior Vice President
Skandinaviska Enskilda Banken

GUNNAR ELIASSON
Chief Economist
Federation of Swedish Industries

ERIK LUNDBERG
Professor of Economics
Stockholm School of Economics

SAM NILSSON
Secretary General, International Federation
of Institutes for Advanced Study (IFIAS)

BENGT RYDEN
President, Business and Social
Research Institute (SNS)

[2]The members of the Swedish group listed here have taken part in the study as private individuals and as experts in the subjects covered. Neither they nor SNS (in accordance with its statutes) are taking a stand on the opinions and recommendations expressed in the statement.

KEIZAI DOYUKAI: Japan Committee for Economic Development

CED Counterpart Organizations in Foreign Countries

Close relationships exist between the Committee for Economic Development and independent, nonpolitical research organizations in other countries. Such counterpart groups are composed of business executives and scholars and have objectives similar to those of CED, which they pursue by similarly objective methods. CED cooperates with these organizations on research and study projects of common interest to the various countries concerned. This program has resulted in a number of joint policy statements involving such international matters as East-West trade, assistance to the developing countries, and the reduction of nontariff barriers to trade.

CEDA	Committee for Economic Development of Australia *128 Exhibition Street, Melbourne, Victoria 3000, Australia*
CEPES	Europäische Vereinigung für Wirtschaftliche und Soziale Entwicklung *56 Friedrichstrasse, Dusseldorf, West Germany*
IDEP	Institut de l'Entreprise *6, rue Clément-Marot, 75008 Paris, France*
経済同友会	Keizai Doyukai (Japan Committee for Economic Development) *Japan Industrial Club Bldg.* *1 Marunouchi, Chiyoda-ku, Tokyo, Japan*
PEP	Political and Economic Planning *12 Upper Belgrave Street, London, SWIX 8BB, England*
SNS	Studieförbundet Näringsliv och Samhälle *Sköldungagatan, 2, 11427 Stockholm, Sweden*

Statements on National Policy
Issued by the Research
and Policy Committee
(publications in print)

---

*International Economic Consequences of High-Priced Energy
  (September 1975)

Broadcasting and Cable Television:
  Policies for Diversity and Change *(April 1975)*

Achieving Energy Independence *(December 1974)*

A New U.S. Farm Policy for Changing World Food Needs *(October 1974)*

Congressional Decision Making for National Security *(September 1974)*

*Toward a New International Economic System:
  A Joint Japanese-American View *(June 1974)*

More Effective Programs for a Cleaner Environment *(April 1974)*

The Management and Financing of Colleges *(October 1973)*

Strengthening the World Monetary System *(July 1973)*

Financing the Nation's Housing Needs *(April 1973)*

Building a National Health-Care System *(April 1973)*

*A New Trade Policy Toward Communist Countries *(September 1972)*

High Employment Without Inflation:
  A Positive Program for Economic Stabilization *(July 1972)*

Reducing Crime and Assuring Justice *(June 1972)*

Military Manpower and National Security *(February 1972)*

The United States and the European Community *(November 1971)*

Improving Federal Program Performance *(September 1971)*

Social Responsibilities of Business Corporations *(June 1971)*

Statements issued in association with CED counterpart organizations in foreign countries.

Education for the Urban Disadvantaged:
   From Preschool to Employment *(March 1971)*

Further Weapons Against Inflation *(November 1970)*

Making Congress More Effective *(September 1970)*

*Development Assistance to Southeast Asia *(July 1970)*

Training and Jobs for the Urban Poor *(July 1970)*

Improving the Public Welfare System *(April 1970)*

Reshaping Government in Metropolitan Areas *(February 1970)*

Economic Growth in the United States *(October 1969)*

Assisting Development in Low-Income Countries *(September 1969)*

*Nontariff Distortions of Trade *(September 1969)*

Fiscal and Monetary Policies for Steady Economic Growth *(January 1969)*

Financing a Better Election System *(December 1968)*

Innovation in Education: New Directions for the American School *(July 1968)*

Modernizing State Government *(July 1967)*

*Trade Policy Toward Low-Income Countries *(June 1967)*

How Low Income Countries Can Advance Their Own Growth *(September 1966)*

Modernizing Local Government *(July 1966)*

A Better Balance in Federal Taxes on Business *(April 1966)*

Budgeting for National Objectives *(January 1966)*

Presidential Succession and Inability *(January 1965)*

Educating Tomorrow's Managers *(October 1964)*

Improving Executive Management in the Federal Government *(July 1964)*

Trade Negotiations for a Better Free World Economy *(May 1964)*

Union Powers and Union Functions: Toward a Better Balance *(March 1964)*

Japan in the Free World Economy *(April 1963)*

Economic Literacy for Americans *(March 1962)*

Cooperation for Progress in Latin America *(April 1961)*

Statements issued in association with CED counterpart organizations in foreign countries.